Managing the Unmanageable

MANAGING
THE
UNMANAGEABLE

Unlock Your Full Management Potential
to Empower Your Top Performers

MIKE CECIL

NEW YORK

LONDON • NASHVILLE • MELBOURNE • VANCOUVER

MANAGING THE UNMANAGEABLE

Unlock Your Full Management Potential to Empower
Your Top Performers

Published in New York, New York, by Morgan James Publishing. Morgan James is a
trademark of Morgan James, LLC. www.MorganJamesPublishing.com

Proudly distributed by Publishers Group West®

A **FREE** ebook edition is available for you
or a friend with the purchase of this print book.

CLEARLY SIGN YOUR NAME ABOVE

Instructions to claim your free ebook edition:
1. Visit MorganJamesBOGO.com
2. Sign your name CLEARLY in the space above
3. Complete the form and submit a photo
   of this entire page
4. You or your friend can download the ebook
   to your preferred device

ISBN 9781636982786 paperback
ISBN 9781636982793 ebook
Library of Congress Control Number:
2023943161

Cover and Interior Design by:
Chris Treccani
www.3dogcreative.net

Morgan James is a proud partner of Habitat for Humanity Peninsula
and Greater Williamsburg. Partners in building since 2006.

Get involved today! Visit: www.morgan-james-publishing.com/giving-back

CONTENTS

AN IMPORTANT WORD BEFORE

We make a living by what we get. We make a life by what we give.

—Winston Churchill

A leader is best when people barely know he exists when his work is done, his aim fulfilled, they will say: we did it ourselves.

—Lao Tzu

My name is Mike Cecil, and I have been—apparently—"unmanageable."

Allow me to give you the particulars of that.

I have worked in the construction industry for over forty-two years. I hold Master's licenses in plumbing, HVAC, gas-fitting, and electrical. The last thirty years have been dedicated to constructing water and wastewater treatment plants.

My last boss fired me, and I was in shock, having never been fired. The abrupt dismissal was done on a phone call, fast and swift. Most shocking about the firing was the fact that I was the rainmaker, who brought in over *$80 million* worth of contracts in the four years I was employed at that firm.

What Was Really Going On

The truth about the story of my firing is that things were going swimmingly for about the last three and a half years, but for several months he kept micromanaging me with things he did not even understand, nor had much experience with other than what I had taught him.

He would often say, "Have you done this, have you done that? You need to do this, and you need to do that." From a person who, before I appeared on the scene, had only done one other design-build project in his career. I taught him what to do and how to win work, and now suddenly he was the expert, and began chiding me on what, in his mind, was my lack of expertise.

What drove him to the point of firing me? I would ask myself. We'd had a few conversations about this previously and he agreed to back off and let me do my thing. But moving forward, he could not help himself and continued the badgering.

On what turned out to be my last day there, I sent him a very polite email, asking him to back off from the micromanaging and to let me do my thing, please.

I read that email on occasion to make sure I was polite and not out of line. I was not. I showed it to my wife, herself a smart business person, and she concurred that I was totally professional. I could only conclude that it was his perception and lack of ability to be in total control that caused his meltdown and knee-jerk reaction.

He flipped out over that email, and the words flew out of his mouth, "I can't work like this. You are fired."

This was truly a control freak in his finest (or worst) hour. He *had to* control his "subservient." The need for power and control had a stronger claim on him than the need to make sound business decisions. At times, poor managers let power go to their head and cannot make logical business decisions. This was a classic case.

Now, I'm sure this guy is worth a lot more money than me, but is that what it's really about? For me, gaining the respect and admiration and loyalty of people is really the end goal.

I can honestly say that I gave my heart and soul into this company, helping it grow. It saddens me the way it ended, but that was beyond my control.

All I have to say about this manager is, "Bless his heart. His loss." He was unable or unwilling to learn how to manage me, the rainmaker. He failed to adapt. He is an engineer and, to put it kindly, could not figure out to make a circle work with a square.

When I started with this company, they were doing about $36 million of yearly sales. In the fourth year of my tenure, sales revenues were about $76 million annually. I was a crucial component in nearly doubling their revenue in four years.

Looking back and analyzing the situation: My boss, co-owner of the company, went to engineering school, not management school. He could not or simply would not figure out how to manage an outlier like me. This is truly his loss. I am a Type-A person who goes at 100 mph. To be a great manager, you need to know how to manage all personalities, especially this type. Not just the "yes" people.

After years of experience managing and being managed, I want to pass onto you what I know are the ways to manage … and the ways *not* to manage … with the hope this will be helpful as you strive for a great and successful working environment.

A Great Manager

People are not robots. We are all made different. To be a great manager or leader of your employees, you need to recognize the differences, strengths, and weaknesses and use that to your advantage. Get out of my way and do not micro-manage.

Business is not family; business is a team. As Michael Gerber says, in my favorite business management book, *The E-Myth Revisited*, "as a manager, you wear different hats."

Tiresome corporate rhetoric loves to say mouth the words, "We are a family." But in business you are not a family; you are a team.

A good manager is like the coach of a team. Is it more successful for the team to adapt to the coach, or for the coach to recognize what talent is in place and put them in the correct position? Someone may be great as a quarterback, but lousy as an offensive lineman.

An ego-driven manager will try to force people into roles and to perform skills they don't possess. Or they become jealous of an employee who outshines and out-performs them.

An ego-driven manager will also let "favorites" get away with murder, while others are held to standards.

Excellent management doesn't allow any team player to run amok and afoul of corporate philosophy or protocol. It cannot be tolerated when there is disrespectful, degrading, dishonest, disengaging, prejudiced, or any other form of unacceptable behavior.

Who's Writing This Book

At one level, the experience of being terminated prompted me to write this book. Why?

Because I know there are many people whose managers don't really know how to manage them. And they feel there is something wrong with them or that they are somehow "doing it all wrong" at work.

I also know there are many managers who really were not trained to be managers, and—in the fray of getting things done—lose sight of or never really knew how to manage.

At another level, I write because my passion is helping people. I believe it's the reason I'm here on this planet. I do much work for charitable organizations and get great satisfaction. I have served on several boards of philanthropic organizations, which gives me great joy.

Not so long ago, before my dismissal, I was in the company's main office and collected my mail. In it was a "thank you" letter from someone in Pittsburgh and I had no idea who it was from. I read it to a few people at work. The writer stated that they were appreciative of the generous gift I bestowed on them and could not wait to see me again. I had no idea who this person was, and it puzzled me.

The two people I read it to, could not pick up any clues. I explained that I always give money away to strangers, and thought maybe the "thank you" resulted from something like that. I was taken aback by the one person saying, "Why would you do that—give money to strangers. I watch my money very closely?"

Why wouldn't you? I thought. We were put on this earth to help people and be kind and generous. I've never seen an armored car following a hearse, because it's true that you can't take it with you. In my experience, I've seen that if you are generous, kind, and loving - somehow, you will always be rewarded and it your goodness to others will come back to you.

As it turned out, the letter came from a couple I'd met at church, knew they were from out of town, and paid for them to have a nice dinner during their visit in the town where they were visiting, I was not expecting any type of thank you. That is not why I do things.

My Roots

I have to give credit where it's due. My values were taught to me by my saintly mother. Whenever she saw a priest or nun, she would give them money.

Now, I always do the same thing wherever I see religious people, no matter the denomination. They make little money and deserve our thanks for making the world a better place. I have always given money equally to priests, nuns, rabbis, or mullahs.

On one of our trips to Rome, my wife said, "Michael, you're outnumbered here and are going to go broke. There are more nuns and priests than you can give money to."

I can honestly say that, because of this open and giving stance toward life and people, I have been beautifully rewarded many times.

… Except when I was summarily fired after doubling a company's cash intake.

Which leads me back to my former boss.

How Some Business Leaders Fail

My former company boss will be losing sales because his pride and ego got in the way of good business judgment and managerial skills. Terminating high achievers and your A-players can often be very costly for managers. Do not let your pride and ego get in the way of making sound business decisions. Check your ego at the door.

I was not disrespectful on my last day, but simply asked him to stop micromanaging me and let me do my job. He could not handle that. I will never forget his last words on the phone: "I can't work like this. You are fired."

I said, "Well, that is a *you* problem. There are plenty of people who could utilize my skillset."

Now the thing is, if you're going to stand up for yourself, you need to be sure of the ground you're standing on. Bragging or overblowing your credentials or experience doesn't cut it.

As it happens, in my eleven-year career in the Business Development world, I have been responsible for $1 billion in sales. For all that effort, I would receive only token bonuses; it was always about the win for me. Granted, on many of those wins, I was just part of a team, but on some I flew solo and did all the work on a proposal.

Most Owners and Managers do not understand how to handle high achievers like me. I am not a maniac, and people consider me kind and empathetic. I do know, from experience, that I have a lot to offer the world and the working environment to make it a better place. I also know, however, that I cannot and will not be micromanaged. It smothers me and takes the wind out of my sails.

Creating a Great Working Environment

If you want to be a great manager, leave your pride and ego home. It has no place at work. I have been in the workplace for over forty-two years. Along the way, I have had great managers, good managers, and terrible managers.

Let's start with ...

Meetings

People like me do not like to attend needless and never-ending meetings.

Good managers should make meetings efficient and no more than 15 to 20 minutes, *not hours,* unless you are laying out an important strategy. And you better have a detailed and well-thought-out agenda to avoid wasting time. We, the employees, are interested in the bottom line and cutting through the baloney.

And here's a thought about ...

Business Teams

I have never been a "yes-person," and I don't know anyone who really likes them. I also have very little patience for the incompetence or laziness of co-workers or employees. The lousy managers surround themselves with robots who agree with everything they say. That's great for the ego, if you have a small one that needs to be constantly propped up, but it's terrible for the bottom line and for keeping your All-Star talent.

In a very funny, animated movie called "Madagascar," the hilarious penguins often say, "Smile and wave, boys. Smile and wave." That's a great picture of yes-people. They just smile and wave—and stay under the radar, when, really, an idea or directive needs to be more closely examined because it may have holes in it.

Surrounding yourself with yes-people creates a toxic atmosphere that limits the potential growth of your company or division and constrains creativity.

Then there is the matter of ...

Retaining Good and Valuable Employees

Retaining good employees, the valuable ones, makes your life simpler and your business much more profitable. The thing is, sometimes you really have to learn how to do it. And that means being open and listening and flexible.

By following the guidelines and advice I and others with years of experience offer, you as a manager will not constantly be putting out fires and hiring the next person who may or may not be a good fit within your organization's skillset.

Employee turnover is expensive, time-consuming, and bad for business and morale. Instead of concentrating on building your business or department, finding good people to replace the person you lost to your competitor becomes a constant struggle.

Retaining good employees is difficult. It is partly art, partly science, and, in a big way, the skill of understanding how people's minds work.

I'm going into a little bit of detail here.

To become a great manager or leader, you should research psychology. What makes different people react to situations, and what makes them tick? There is no magic formula. Depending on the generation, the practices and techniques will differ from baby boomers, millennials, Gen X to Gen Y.

Hiring replacement employees because you don't know how to manage the ones you have is *not* the optimum growth strategy. It costs an exorbitant amount of time, money, and effort, while also disrupting the usual daily activities of trying to run a business and being profitable. Face it: it's is a hassle.

Retaining good employees is not vastly different from keeping loyal customers. It is easy to maintain customers (if you give good service) but tricky, costly, and time-consuming to bring new customers on board. Your life will be much simpler and more accessible if competent and loyal employees stay with you.

Retaining great employees saves companies a lot of precious time and money while also creating a better work environment for everyone. Outstanding management means excellent employee retention and greater profitability.

Then there's this ...

A Manager Needs Self-Awareness

Being a poor or ineffective manager makes your life harder and your business less profitable. Unfortunately, most substandard managers have little self-awareness and do not even realize they are. Their employees are too worried about keeping their job to say anything. They have little self-awareness.

By following some simple rules, one can be an excellent manager that people want to work with. It is not difficult but does require patience and fortitude as well as a keen level of self-awareness and a bit of humility. I promise you that by following the guidelines offered in this book, people will want to work with you and they will be loyal to a fault.

Not That Complicated

In fact, there is a very simple formula for being a great manager.

First, be empathetic towards your employees and coworkers. People thrive when they know their bosses and coworkers truly care about them as a person and not just an employee.

Second, treat them well. There are some simple tips below for how to do that.

Third, learn about them and their family. It only takes a few minutes a week but it can mean the world to them. I firmly believe that developing a personal relationship with your coworkers and/or employees builds bonds and trusting relationships. Showing interest is a very simple relationship builder. But you must be genuine in this. People see beyond fake interest, snake oil, and baloney.

If you're honest, trustworthy and authentic with your coworkers and employees, they, in turn, will trust you and have the confidence to go above and beyond and make your company a better place.

TAKEAWAY

Here are some straightforward tips for retaining your top talent.

- Pay them well
- Treat them well
- Leave them alone
- Utilize golden handcuff strategies
- Give them skin in the game
- Share the wealth

By following these tips, you will retain your best employees. They will be more productive, more satisfied with their work and be extremely loyal to you and the company. This will improve your company's bottom line and create a pleasant work environment.

LESSON 2

The Sheeples

What every manager wants is workers who add to the well-being of the organization—even if it means challenging them in a constructive way, drawing upon their skills and know-how to shape the plans of management.

However.

Businesses are plagued by "sheeples"—that is, people who are not confident in their skills or abilities and just want to keep their job without making any waves.

They are docile, foolish, or easily led. They are unable to think for themselves and have few cognitive abilities.

Unlike these low performers, high performers will not put up with the garbage when managers won't listen when a better way to do things is laid out. They will move onto greener pastures to a place where they can spread their wings and thrive.

In my experience, the problem of keeping on sheeples, because they are yes-people, and resisting the efforts of high performers is unfortunately wide-spread. More than many managers would admit.

So I want to focus on the problem of sheeples a bit more.

Why?

Because if you're a manager, you need to see what's clogging the systems of your company.

Who Are They

Sheeples are intellectually lazy and unmotivated. This does not mean they are unintelligent. They can sound perfectly brilliant. But—here's the thing—they have no drive to seek out differing points of view to discover the full set of facts about a given matter. They follow the crowd like sheep (thus the term for them).

Why do I say they're intellectually lazy? Because sheeples get their news from one source without, as I mentioned, looking at multiple sources to garner a consensus of facts or opinions about a matter. We see them on social media—those who do not do any fact-checking.

They voluntarily acquiesce to a suggestion without critical analysis or research. Those who want to manipulate them know that stupid sells better than genius. The reason stupidity sells so well is because people who don't think flock towards positions and beliefs that are not thought out but are based in bias and emotion because they are familiar and safe and offer the easiest path.

I had a very dear friend who would post things on Facebook. She, in her case, a a hardcore Republican and never ever did any independent research. Even if I agreed with the article, I would call her out on "news" that was clearly false and could easily, with the least bit of research, be proven untrue. I am amazed at how people think, "If it's on the internet it must be true," as did my friend.

Finding Out Who They Are

All organizations have sheeples, and they are easy to recognize and easy to manipulate. Use that to your advantage.

High performers do not like following all the rules, being micro-managed, or adhering to a strict regimen. They are usually the type who check sources, do not follow the crowd, and are independent of the masses.

Retaining your top performers is crucial to a profitable business. Sheeples are about 80 percent of your workforce in pretty much any industry. Ignore them and concentrate on the high performers.

TAKEAWAY

- Identify the sheeples within your organization; they are easy to spot. Do not promote them beyond their abilities or talent levels.

- Understand that you will not be able to change them; don't waste your time. They have worked their entire life to become what they are. You are their manager, not their life coach or psychologist.

- Utilize most of your time and effort on the high achievers, who in turn will make your business more profitable.

Effective Communication

Have you ever listened to a business leader make a presentation and wondered,

What the heck is he (or she) talking about?

Great leaders communicate clearly and concisely. Clear communication skills are essential to becoming a successful manager. Why?

Because it builds trust.

It is detrimental to the organization and its overall success when management fails to communicate effectively.

Communication happens in many ways. Let's look at some of the ones that are important to your role as leader.

Types of Communication

Nonverbal

To communicate effectively, be aware of your body language, posture, and tone of voice. It is essential to make eye contact with your audience.

Provide feedback through nonverbal ways such as nodding your head and an open body posture. Body language builds rapport and trust.

Make Eye Contact

Eye contact activates the limbic mirror system, meaning when you share eye contact with people, the same neurons firing in someone's brain will also fire in yours. This is the foundation of trust and understanding.

Making eye contact helps you to have more focus on the conversation. You are better able to read facial expressions, which in turn improves understanding. Make fleeting and non-intrusive glances. This assists with bonding and increases empathy and honesty.

Facial Expressions

Smile. Be happy and interested. When you are glad and focused on them, people instantly sense it by means of your facial expressions, and this will put them at ease.

We can instantly sense the mood of someone with their facial expression, whether it is happiness, sadness, fear, anger, or empathy.

When conversing, display the correct facial expression corresponding to the topic at hand. It is not a one-size-all proposition. Depending on the nature of the conversation, your expressions may be happiness, disappointment, seriousness, or other tones.

Gestures

Use hand gestures to illustrate your point or a simple nod of the head to show that you are paying attention.

Consider these types of hand gestures:

- *Sweeping outward*: indicates a welcome.
- *Sweeping inward*: shows inclusiveness and collectiveness, communicating that "we are in this together and as a team."
- *Hands on your heart*: signals that something is vital to you.
- *Use your right hand and left hand* to demonstrate the message, "On the one hand we have this, but on the other hand we have that."
- *Pointing*: NEVER do this; it is rude. Instead, clench your hand and have your thumb outside of the clench and point with your thumb. Observe how most politicians do this.

- *Bringing your hands together* in a prayerlike fashion or clenching your hands together shows that we are coming together on something.

Showing if something is big or small by *big or small gestures* helps to indicate it is of little importance or could have a significant impact and is of great importance.

I highly recommend reading *Do's and Don'ts: Hand Gestures When Public Speaking* by Teresa Zumwalt.

Also, watch some TED Talks and notice successful people presenting. TED Talk speakers use many hand gestures to communicate their message and emphasize specific points. This takes practice to be effective.

Using Your Whole Being and Demeanor to Communicate

Posture and Body Orientation

This is very subliminal, and you may not even know what signals you may be sending. One needs to study this to ensure you are sending the right message. Some studies have shown that speech only makes up from 20 percent to 30 percent of communication, with eye contact and body language being a more powerful force.

An open and closed posture reflects an individual's degree of confidence or receptivity to another person. If in a closed position, one may have their arms folded, legs crossed or positioned at a slight angle from the person they are communicating with.

Humor

Everyone enjoys a little humor but be careful to make it tasteful and suited for your audience. Nothing crude. Ever. Humor can help create a healthy workplace and unify the team, releasing tensions. Employees may be less likely to leave a workplace with a fun atmosphere.

Silence

It is often difficult to be silent during conversations, but make it a practice to have reflectively pauses and allow your superiors or employees time to speak. As Marcus Tullius Cicero said, "Silence is one of the great arts of conversation."

A brief interlude of silence in conversations allows one to process what someone just said. Pause for a few seconds after someone speaks to help you fully absorb what they said.

Silence enables one to think of good questions by being more thoughtful and the next question.

Silence slows down the pace of a conversation and allows it to become more meaningful. It is in our nature to want to speak without listening. Short pauses enable you to focus on an exchange and become more thoughtful about the subject and your audience.

Communication Channels

Be aware of the potential effects of the method you use to communicate your message.

Email may be acceptable for sharing with a large group of employees but may not be adequate to get a piece of important news to an individual or small group.

Communicate *face-to-face* when possible. There is a chance that emails can be misinterpreted, even with the best of intentions. In-person communication allows one to use gestures and smiles (or frowns) to communicate your message.

Pick up the phone, or better yet, *visit* your employees in person and have a chat about non-work-related things. It builds trust and boosts morale. It demonstrates to them that you care about them as a person and the unique human being that they are. Always remember that their lives matter.

Finessing Your Communication Style

Work at it. Here's how.

Leave your ego home

I worked for a massive construction company many years ago, and the President (Mr. P) of the company always made a point to go around the office at least once a week and talk to his employees, even if it was to say *hi* and *thanks*.

If Mr. P did have an ego, it certainly did not show. Everyone had the utmost respect for this man. He demonstrated that he cared. The company had a remarkably high retention rate. People stayed because they felt like they were part of a Team, and it was not uncommon for people to spend their entire careers with this firm.

Mr. P would visit my project sites about twice a year. While he was a very kind, empathetic, and brilliant man, one had better know their project details, or you would not last long.

He would question the Project Manager and Superintendent on just about every item on a budget, equipment, or labor report and you'd better have every number memorized. I was told he would read the project reports in the company plane on the way to the project sites and remember all the numbers.

If Mr. P asked *why* you were doing something a certain way and you replied, "Because that's the way I've always done it," you would not be around for long. Your response better be good. And if you did not have an answer to his question, you had best not reply, "I don't know." Your response had to be, "I am not sure right now, Mr. P, but I'll do some research and have an answer for you no later than tomorrow."

Mr. P let you know what his expectations were, and you knew you better be always on you're A-Game. He did not expect perfection but rather excellence.

Let me add, *small gestures* can mean a lot. I knew Mr. P liked to drink Dr. Pepper. So, I always had a six-pack of this beverage in the refrigerator in case of a surprise visit. He was greatly pleased by this and said I was the only one who ever had Dr. Pepper available. Sometimes, it's the little things in life that bring great joy.

As a result of his hands-on, detail-focused management style—and his expectation that we actually know our jobs, the company enjoyed a high retention rate. That undoubtedly saved an exorbitant number of resources instead of constantly hiring people and training them. Mr. P had built a cohesive team, and for the most part, everyone was a team player and glad to be part of this dynamic organization.

Be Genuine

Most people can see through you and know if you are sincere. Coming across as honest may take some time to master—eye contact. Don' stare, that gives people the creeps, but occasionally looking the person directly in the eye without making them nervous.

Listen, Listen, Listen

It is crucial to listen. It is challenging for many people to truly listen. Genuine listening is problematic because it is our natural urge to want to continue talking or to be thinking about our response rather than being attentive to what the other is saying.

Pay careful attention when someone else is speaking. Imagine there will be a test at the end of the conversation and try to soak up as much information as possible. Listening prepares you for a conversation, allowing you to formulate adequate responses in a discussion.

In fact, a good measure of your success in the workplace includes active listening. When you actively listen, your employees can see the difference between you and others, notice you pay attention to them, and genuinely care.

Active listening also includes body language. As mentioned before, you will be saying much without saying a word by nodding your head, making eye contact, and smiling.

Active listening is not easy and requires much focus and a conscious effort to master. It builds trust. If you truly pay attention when another is speaking, it will help you retain the information transmitted to you. You will remember the conversation much better and gain knowledge and understanding.

When listening to a conversation, provide active verbal feedback to encourage the speaker to continue and show them you are paying attention.

Meaningful Eye Contact

The eyes are the window to the soul and making eye contact casually and comfortably builds trust. It is a learned skill.

Making direct eye contact will be different for every person. Certain people just do not like eye contact and may get nervous or uncomfortable. After a few meetings with your employees, you will begin to know when and how much eye contact to make, so the person does not feel uncomfortable.

Nonetheless, some amount of eye contact is essential and shows the other person that you genuinely pay attention and think the conversation is essential, valuing what they have to say.

Getting Help

Ask your manager or partner or a close friend for constructive feedback about your communication skills. Here are some questions that help you improver your communication skills.

- Did you feel I was giving you my undivided attention?
- Did I make enough or too much eye contact?
- Did I make you feel comfortable or uncomfortable?
- How was my tone? Was it too loud, soft, or demanding?
- Did I allow you enough time for your part of the conversation? Did I interrupt you at all?
- Did I show you the respect you deserve?

Do not hesitate to get feedback from a peer, boss, or employee. If you ask them to do so, the input will help you with further conversations. There is nothing to be ashamed about in receiving constructive criticism. It is the only way to learn, grow, and become the best—to become the manager and leader you strive to be.

When making crucial or casual conversations, it is of the utmost importance to turn off your cell phone or office phone. Take the few minutes a conversation will take and give your undivided attention.

Speaking of crucial conversations, there is a wonderfully insightful book called—as you might guess—*Crucial Conversations*, by Kerry Patterson and a few co-authors, which was required reading for me during my professional development. I recommend this great read, as you are sure to garner tremendous value from implementing the techniques found within. It can significantly help you with your ability to deal with difficult employees or delicate conversations.

In *Crucial Conversations*, the authors illustrate how you can handle difficult conversations when the stakes are high, with strong emotions and varying opinions on a matter. Their techniques outline how to transform anger and hurt feelings into robust dialogue and make it safe to talk about almost anything.

No Gossip

Your employees and co-workers will think you are more credible and trustworthy if you avoid gossip or speak ill of someone else. Just do not do it and stay away from this pettiness. It is poison in any environment, especially the workplace. Gossip causes disruption and inhibits productivity. It is your duty and responsibility to ensure gossip will not be tolerated. Period.

People who gossip thrive on drama and conflict. The root cause of gossip is jealousy, usually perpetrated by insecure people. Mostly, people that promote gossip are short on responsibility. Get rid of them—they spread toxins. They create an unhealthy environment, which kills morale.

What to do instead ...

Provide Feedback

Weak managers do not provide good feedback. Giving feedback is a critical element of becoming a great manager. It is not easy. If the input about an employee is negative, it can make the situation very uncomfortable and, more importantly, not help get the job done. Whenever possible, *offer constructive* criticism:

"Here's what's not working" can be followed with, "Here's what may work better" or "Let's talk about ways to make this work better."

Sometimes constructive criticism isn't possible. Then, you should remember that ven what may be considered negative feedback can help someone in their career if they're savvy enough to accept it and want to improve

Feedback does not cost money and provides the best possible workplace communication.

Whether positive, negative, or constructive, feedback gives employees a sense of confidence to further their careers and become the best they can be. Great managers who constantly and consistently provide feedback display confidence and, through this level of communication, get to know their employees better.

While the word "criticism" connotes negativity, it's an excellent way to promote employee development and improvement. How will one learn to become better or more proficient if no one reflects back to them their strengths and areas where they still need to grow? anything to them?

Finally, when providing criticism of any kind, be firm but fair.

The fact is, we all need other people to help us see how the world views us, helping us to step outside our myopic vision of ourselves.

I once had one boss whom I did not think could *ever* provide positive feedback. I believe he felt that if you still had a job and he did not fire you, then you were doing great. Do not be that leader. Be better than that. When you provide any kind of feedback, most of all, be sincere. Show them that you genuinely care about them as a person and that you truly want them to succeed and what you're promoting is excellence.

While it's not always possible, depending on the nature of the feedback, try to ensure that it's tied to a measurable goal.

Make Goals Clear and Attainable

Which is to say, make the development of excellence measurable and not just esoteric. Strive for goals that are achievable, but not an easy slam-dunk. If your goal is forty-something, then strive for fifty-something. And remember that if you set goals too high, you risk turning conscientiousness into apathy.

Suppose a salesperson increases sales from 20 percent to 30 percent. Tell them you are pleased and tell them that senior management has noticed and has been offering high praise for them and their work.

Communication builds confidence and makes an employee want to strive to beat any goal. Make it worth their while to excel and bring in more business or clients. The employee should be vested in both the input as to how the job is done and in the outcome. Share the success.

The same is applicable for any industry or trade, such as attorneys, salespeople, or accountants who bring in more clients than their peers or beat their projections or billable hours.

TAKEAWAY

A great manager is a great communicator. This is key to success. Of all the topics aforementioned, the most important can be summed up as follows:

- Be genuine.
- Eye contact is extremely important.
- Do not limit conversations to strictly topics that are work-related. Talk about things outside of the workplace, so people can see how you are as a real person—one who authentically cares about them.

LESSON 4

Be Accountable and Responsible

Great leaders accept accountability for their decisions and actions and do not try to pass the blame when something goes south. Being accountable builds respect among employees and co-workers.

Do Not Be Like This Guy

I once worked under a manager (Mr. M) who would regularly throw his subordinates under the bus for anything that went wrong. The fault or failure was never his. He never accepted accountability for his actions.

Few people liked or respected Mr. M except the other sheeple at the firm, who also did not take responsibility and routinely blamed others.

Mr. M's behavior eventually caught up with him. Senior management became aware that he was not cut out for a management position. Accountability starts at the top. The buck stops there. If you are a senior leader or owner of a company, it begins with you.

Accountability is paramount in building a successful company or division within a firm. Accountability improves employee performance, satisfaction, morale, innovation, and trust. A lack of accountability erodes trust.

Think about people you have worked with or went to school with who always shirked accountability for their actions. I suspect the person who comes to mind is someone you would not trust. Trust is everything. Without trust, there is no foundation because we have little faith in people that are not trustworthy.

People who are not trustworthy do not pass what I call, *The Foxhole Test*. It builds bare-minimum mindsets. It reduces productivity and contributes to building terrible habits. Accountability needs to be judged by what is measurable and counted.

Did you fail to reach your sales goal? Did you lose a client? Did you lose a bid? While the word accountability may seem abstract, it is usually tied to something measurable.

Be accountable and take responsibility for your decisions, especially the ones that lead to a failure on behalf of your organization We are all human and will make some bad decisions. Occasionally making poor decisions is expected and part of the process.

So, admit your mistake(s), learn your lesson, and move on. If you have never made a wrong decision, you are playing it too safe. You are too scared. A wise investor once said, "Scared money does not make money."

It may seem like I'm talking to people down-line, but I'm talking to managers. Some managers try to blame others for problems so they don't look bad in front of their superiors. Don't be that person. Own up to it if you've dropped the ball. Overall, it will serve you better if top people see that you're willing to be accountable and learn from your missteps.

Long-Term Thinking

Always have the long game in mind, not just short-term gains. Too many companies are concerned about quarterly earnings and immediate profits; they often fail to look at the big picture and are reliant on how short-term gains may affect the overall strategy and progress of a firm.

Look at people like Elon Musk, Steve Jobs, and Jeff Bezos. They have/had incredible long-term thinking and helped build successful empires.

Bezos is spending $42 million of his own money to build a 10,000-year clock. Now that is long-term thinking! When you focus on the future, you will naturally create a plan and map a blueprint for achieving your long-term goals.

It is essential to have a long-term plan. Without knowing where you are going, it is impossible to be prepared for how you will get there. Making short-term profits is a necessity for a business to survive. Still, you must not ignore the improvement of yourself and your employees for your business or division's long-term strategy and growth.

If you are not constantly innovating and improving, you will soon be out of the game because your competitors will be doing just that and surpassing you in all areas.

Warren Buffett has some great things to say regarding long-term investing: "Stick with long-term value investing strategies. Don't let fear and greed change your investing criteria and values."

The same holds with running a business and being a good manager. It would be best if you had concrete long-term goals and a detailed plan for getting there.

It is recommended, nay, I believe essential, that you develop a one-year, three-year, and five-year plan for your division or business, outlining your goals and objectives. In my long career, I have been involved in many executive management retreats, usually held yearly, to build or expand upon a long-term company strategy.

You can envision what the company or department will look like or deserve in 10 years. Use measurable goals.

Do Your Homework

There is homework to do before your long-term planning retreats. Do not just show up and expect anything to be accomplished. If you are a manager or senior leader, you must give out assignments a few weeks before the planning retreat to get the best bang for your buck and the most thought-provoking and productive meeting.

This practice builds a sense of camaraderie and makes you closer to your peers while also creating a sense of trust. Without a strong sense of confidence, your business or company will flounder, and growth will stagnate.

> Remember that people like to work with people they trust.

An atmosphere of trust helps to avoid or eliminate excessive oversight that can inhibit innovation and slow progress. Trust creates transparency in a workplace and increases productivity. I cannot stress enough the importance of trust.

In my role as a Director of Business Development, I found that there is a formula for winning the project. Namely, clients select people they like, know, trust, and who deliver as promised. This is the formula and the key to success. A sense of faith and the client having confidence in your abilities will beat a fancy brochure or presentation any day.

My Philosophy Is to Outwork and Out-Think My Competitors

On one long-term planning retreat in which about twenty-five people were in attendance, the group did a few team-building exercises, and, at one point, we completed *Hermann's Whole Brain Model* test, developed by Ned Hermann, a remarkable man.

I recommend having your employees take this test.

Alternatively, there is the Myers-Briggs or other similar brain model tests, to guide and provide insight to identify personal traits which can assist managers and employees in developing to their best potential. It is often enlightening to determine their most vital characteristics for building the best success within their skill set.

If you are unfamiliar with *Hermann's Whole Brain Model Test*, there are four quadrants. The two on the left are *A. Facts* and *B. Form.*

Whole Brain Model™

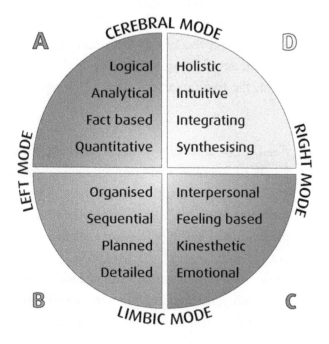

A. *Facts* (a greater tendency toward analytical thinking) indicates you are logical, technical, or financial. Typical for engineers, bankers, attorneys, scientists, and accountants.

A-quadrant thinkers prefer quantifying, analyzing, theorizing and processing logically.

B. *Form* (practically/pragmatically oriented) indicates that you are organized, and plan-, detail-, and business-focused.

This type of person is similar the person oriented to Facts, and works well in careers such as accounting, engineering, banking, attorneys, schedulers, actuaries, and some entrepreneurs. B-Quadrant thinkers prefer organizing, sequencing, evaluating and practicing. On the right, the two quadrants are *C. Feelings* and *D. Futures.*

C. *Feelings* (relationally oriented) indicates intense levels of interpersonal connectedness, emotionally savvy, and willingness to help. Typically, these are teachers, counselors, artists, salespeople, and the like. People who want to assist others.

D. *Futures* (or experimental) indicate an integrative personality, strong imagination, insightful person, and a visionary. Many are social workers, teachers, psychologists, artists, designers, and the like.

Most participants in my exercise were engineers, estimators, project managers, bean counters, and superintendents Very technically competent. Almost all the people in the room were way off on the left quadrant.

This made much sense based on their job assignments and specialties.

My personal chart showed very little penetration into the A and B left-side quadrants, which are logical, numbers-based, and fact-based. I was about as far to the right as possible, with *Futures* and *Feelings* both highly dominant.

As the group discussed the results, it was apparent that only two people in the room were extremely far to the right side, with *Feelings* and *Futures* being highly dominant—the Human Resources Director and me. She was a wonderful person, and we got along splendidly. "Well, I guess that confirms it," I proudly exclaimed. "I'm a female! I suspected it, but now I have scientific proof."

The truth is, I am an emotional person and very okay with that. I am not scared or embarrassed to cry in front of someone. Who cares? Real men are not afraid to cry. In my early career, I was a rough and tough construction worker lugging around a 90-pound jackhammer—a skinny, 150-pound frame of a man who could carry his weight. But we cannot change who we are deep inside. (A story on that later.)

The point of the brain test exercise and similar tests is to get different personality types working together to foster creativity. If an organization has all left-sided quadrants working together, there will be minimal creativity or long-term strategy and planning. There needs to be a balance between optimizing the best workplace results.

Making It All Work Together

Modeling employees' personalities and strong traits is an excellent tool for building cohesive teams with different viewpoints, skill sets, and perspectives for conquering complex challenges at an optimal level. If you do so, however, you should share the results with the individuals and not the group unless everyone agrees that is not an issue.

There should be a balance of right-brain and left-brain people for optimum results within any organization. Right-sided people need Left-sided people and vice versa. This makes for the best mix of skills and personalities to bring optimum results within any organization.

Left-sided people are very analytical and typically do not have a clear vision of where a company should go in the long term. If your company has all or primarily right-side quadrant people working together, things can go awry, as there may be no one to keep order.

For these reasons, I encourage you to conduct a brain model test to determine the ideal working group for the most exceptional order and creativity for your business or organization.

TAKEAWAY

In any organization, there needs to be a mix of A & B Quadrants (Left Brain) and C & D Quadrants (Right Brain) to maximize the effectiveness of a group.

By having a balanced mix, it brings about order within a group as well as fostering creativity.

Incentives

I have been de-incentivized in the workplace by bosses who would constantly yell at me. Not a very encouraging workplace. Granted that this was in the construction industry in which men thought they had to have bravado and show their superiority. Not a team atmosphere, but more like being ruled by a dictator.

One particularly extremely profitable project in which we greatly exceeded our profit goal. The way the company bonus structure was set up, is they had a cap on the percentage amount for project bonuses. We reached the maximum bonus and were no longer incentivized to make more money for the company. They could have made more money if there were no cap. This makes no sense to me.

One company I worked for had a lucrative bonus structure for every project I won. It was very encouraging and helped to drive me to work harder to win a project, so I could better take care of my family.

There are mixed feelings about this within the industry. On the one hand, it should all be about the company; however, nothing motivates people like being generously compensated for a job well done and bringing in work.

There is a fine line between just bringing in work for the sake of getting a bonus versus ensuring you are bringing in profitable work. Some people may try to win a project at any cost just to receive an award bonus, even though they may realize it may not be profitable for the company. A solution to this would be to tie an award bonus to the profitability of the project.

This is tricky business in that if you brought in a project but the project did not make projected profit because the "C team" was managing it, that would be out of your control. There is no easy answer on how to solve this.

Achievers

There are two main types of high achievers: 1) Those motivated by money and 2) those motivated by winning.

Your job is to figure out what drives them. Is it money, or is it winning and receiving praise and recognition?

This leads to an important management tenet.

Manage the Person

If a high achiever is primarily finance-motivated, then you are on notice. But how do you manage and retain a potential talent for the highest price without upsetting the pay scale of the company? People talk, gossip, and brag. There are few secrets within any firm.

Not upsetting the general salary ranges can be overcome by setting your A-Players base salaries somewhat higher (top of the scale) than the lesser achievers while also awarding those people in other ways on a goal-oriented bonus structure.

Incentive rewards do not have to be in cash or stocks. Instead, it can be through other perks such as a vehicle, vacation trips to exotic places, golf outings, paying for their daughter's wedding, a fishing trip, paying off student loans - whatever - be creative and get to know what floats their boat. Find out what the person likes, their interests, or hobbies, and tailor an award or incentive that is personal and dear to their heart.

Perhaps they enjoy golf. I gave a reward for a job well done in the form of tickets to watch the Masters Tournament in Augusta, Georgia. One employee loved horses and horse racing, and I purchased them a choice between a fantastic memorable trip to the Kentucky Derby, Preakness, or Belmont Stakes.

Do Not Go Cheap

Rewards will pay you back tenfold. I suggest offering first-class tickets—one of life's joys. (I used to fly so much that I frequently got bumped up to first class if seats were available. I could never see myself paying for that luxury as I have always been cautious with the company funds, but when I did fly first class, it was so lovely and I treasured those flights. Few things are more pleasing than being on the second level of a 747-400!)

In the grand scheme of things, the amount of money it will cost to provide your best people with attractive non-cash bonuses is peanuts against the bottom line. In thinking about people motivated by money and material possessions, rewards and incentives are a tangible way to the retention and for them to continue performing at a top level. These techniques lead to success.

Set up a lucrative bonus structure. The nature of it will depend on what type of business you are involved with and how it is structured.

Companies must have the philosophy of sharing success by spreading wealth.

Whereas not being charitable creates resentment in any organization.

"Pigs get fat and hogs go to slaughter," my Grandma Rosie used to say.

Grandma Rosie was a wonderful lady who ran the farm, managed the Cecil country store, was the butcher, and was the town Post Mistress for over fifty years. The most remarkable lady I have ever known would get my butt out of bed at 5:30 a.m. to slop the hogs. And she made the best scrapple and pork sausage in Saint Mary's County, Maryland.

Everyone loved Grandma Rosie. If you have never had scrapple and want to know the ingredients: "Lips and Assholes." Nothing goes to waste from a hog.

What her homey little saying meant was this:

If you were piggish and hoglike and didn't share—you were still destined to become scrapple.

Bonus structures and incentives will differ for every type of organization, and you will need to crunch some numbers to determine the best business decision on what makes sense against the bottom line.

Take a Close Look

Doing a bit of simple math, let us surmise that your high achiever brings in a new client or project of $1 million worth of goods or services in which you would typically realize a 10 percent *net* profit margin. The company realizes $100,000 in gross profit. Why not structure a bonus of 10 percent of the net or 1 percent of the gross? That is $10,000 of incentive.

I suggest they receive 5 percent of the *net* profit as their bonus structure. Your firm is still making 9 percent. This is industry-specific, and you must determine what is ideal for your business. The point is to reward handsomely so that you can retain the talent.

Good managers understand the importance of the Rainmakers. Without high achievers bringing in the business, there is no business. A-Players work the street and use their relationships and skills to get new business or clients.

Golden Handcuffs

This strategy primarily works in a company or firm that is tangible, empirically based and has goals that can be quantified.

Pay 15 percent or more above your competitors in the industry or practice area.

Devise a handsome bonus system as follows:

- Determine the salary. Often the Rule of Three works here. If you are paying $100,000 to an employee, they should be producing $300,000 in revenue.
- Develop a bonus structure that amounts to X over $300,000. They will be given a Y bonus. This encourages performance.
- Pay the bonus the following calendar year in equal installments.
- Have a two-sentence contract signed yearly by the employee. If you leave, you forfeit your bonus. It is that simple and does not need to be complicated.

This is a very effective and fair strategy. Let us surmise that an economically dominant high achiever receives an offer in July for an extra $25,000 salary. You stand an excellent chance they will not leave because they will be forfeiting 50 percent of their bonus from last year, and they are already still looking forward to next year's bonus.

When someone thinks they will be losing $40,000 in bonus for a $25,000/year pay raise, they will stay.

The Negotiators

Mind you, some high-achieving players will want or perhaps demand a higher percentage of the gross or net profits. This is strictly a business decision to examine. It may be likely that your competitor might compensate them a few percentage points higher, which might entice them to leave your firm.

You will need to weigh and thoroughly consider the options to make an intelligent business decision about whether it is worth it. Or, as my brother, a very successful attorney, is fond of saying, "Is the juice worth the squeeze?" Sometimes you must let the free agent go on about their merry way. After some time, they often realize that the grass is not greener on the other side and may ask to return.

If an employee is solely driven by money, they will likely leave at some point. As the saying goes: "Money Talks and bull crap walks." If your structure is set up to make that a hard decision, you have performed your job as a manager. Often, there is little in the way of company loyalty with people whose primary driver is money. So be keenly aware and know what makes them tick.

Those who are motivated by winning still want to be, and should be, adequately compensated. Remember that they are driven more by winning, titles, praise, and recognition. These are your perfect employees, who sometimes may be challenging to manage. They are free spirits. One of their mottos is, "Second place means being the first loser."

They are the consummate *unmanageables*.

For employees who are your top achievers, making them a vice president or giving a similar title can provide satisfaction, a sense of belonging, and create a willingness to stay.

Titles cost the company nothing, other than the rules governing corporations, but can mean the world to this type of person.

Stock options may be reasonable if you work for a publicly traded company. For the most part, it is deferred compensation and may be a good alternative instead of bonuses or salary increases. As a retention tool, the stock options vest at 20 percent each year after they are awarded.

Most of your high achievers are free-thinkers, who crave independence and autonomy. This is of utmost importance to this type of person, frequently more so than compensation. They think differently than most employees. You need to get into their head and learn how they feel and understand what motivates them and provides satisfaction within the workplace.

Understand This

The A-Player cowboys and cowgirls are not fond of rules, complex structuring, or company policies and procedures. Learn how to navigate around this. As the manager of your band of unmanageable merry misfits, you must know the art of managing. You may need to bend the rules a little. Nothing illegal or immoral is ever to be tolerated, but you can work in the gray.

Many employees want or need structure or a set of systems and procedures but, as I said, not this type of person. You *need* this type of person, however, for your company to thrive and become profitable. Your organization should not primarily have a herd of rule-following robots who are incapable of thinking creatively and whose primary concern is keeping their jobs and staying under the radar.

Skirting company rules is not easy in many organizations. If your business is highly structured with many rules and procedures, you will most likely be unable to retain this type of person in the long run, and as a result, your business may suffer.

One of my favorite books is *First, Break All the Rules: What the World's Greatest Managers Do Differently*, by Marcus Buckingham. The premise of the book and its philosophy acknowledges that high performers who do not appreciate rules need to do their own thing in order to thrive. I recommend reading this delightful book to understand further how our minds work.

Whether these "over the line" types of employees are motivated by money or by the win, a commonality between them is the need for attention, self-worth, and praise. They love to be in the limelight and receive congratulations and recognition both in private and in front of others.

A study completed many years ago by the Dale Carnegie organization found that only 29 percent of employees were fully engaged in their work, with 26 percent fully disengaged and the rest falling between the two extremes.

Other studies have demonstrably illustrated that employees' level of engagement directly correlates with their relationship with their direct supervisor. What matters to them is the praise they receive from their manager, not necessarily the company.

Receiving praise from a direct supervisor changes the mental outlook of an employee, makes the person feel good and shows that their efforts are being noticed. The price of praise is free, but too many lousy managers do not utilize this powerful tool to their detriment and that of their organization.

Be on a first-name basis between you and your staff. An essential thing in the world to any individual is their name. Say it, spell it correctly!

Star Trek?

A shining example of someone who did not like to follow conventional wisdom, or a bunch of meaningless rules (in his mind) was the illustrious Captain James T. Kirk. He was perhaps the best fictional captain ever. I recently watched a "Star Trek Discovery" movie, and one part hit me like a brick. I told myself, "Captain Kirk—he is exactly like me!"

In a scene at the movie's beginning, he was severely chastised and demoted by the Admiral for not following Star Fleet protocol. As the story continues, the Admiral re-instated him because Earth desperately needed someone with guts, his particular skill set, and a total lack of fear to avoid war with the Klingon Empire and save Earth.

You would be too fortunate to have a Captain Kirk in your organization. Just let them save the Earth and do not bind them up and stifle their creativity with needless rules, regulations, and procedures that slow them down and frustrate them. The "Captain Kirks" do not appreciate it, nor will they perform as well as when they are just left alone to work their magic.

Sidebar: About Expenses

Keep expense reports simple. If you want a rule followed, simplify it to bare necessity. One company I was with had the most complicated expense report system in the history of the world, which some crazed bean-counter must have invented.

I had relatively high monthly expenses from my traveling, business lunches, dinners, and entertainment. I dreaded doing this and completing it took me a full day or longer every month. This was a wasteful loss of time when I could have been productive in bringing in more projects or meeting with clients. It served no purpose other than to satisfy some accountant. Who, by the way, never had to travel and never had to do an expense report?

(*Rule number 1 of business travel:* Never let anyone else make your reservations, or you will have two layovers and stay in some crappy hotel room.)

A great thing about one company I was with was the ease of doing the monthly expense report. I did not need to show receipts, and they trusted that all expenses were legitimate. It took only an hour or so to complete, and I found this to be a great relief from previous experiences. There are several programs in the marketplace to track expenses and the ability to use your phone to take pictures of receipts which work well.

TAKEAWAY
- Know what motivates.
- Be generous in your rewards.
- Make it clear that the reward is for meeting set goals.
- Make it clear what an additional reward is, if they exceed the goal by X percent.

LESSON 6

What NOT to Do with Self-Motivated People

Your All-Stars are self-motivated and do not need to be micro-managed. They are your A-Players and thrive when given their independence and flexibility.

Highly motivated people are essential for your business growth and success. My philosophy is in direct opposition to conventional thinking. Most managers spend most of their time on low-performing employees.

Many managers feel they need to help the marginal employees and low performers. They are constantly putting out fires or training the untrainable. Unmotivated people can be like a flat tire to your team. Low motivation can spread within an organization, sucking the life out of a company and bringing morale down for everyone.

My advice is to do the opposite and spend more time with the motivated.

Some managers are reluctant to do what I suggest, because they are insecure and afraid that the high performers may take their management position and rise above them.

If such is the case, they are not good managers or leaders and possibly have issues with their confidence level. You need to examine your team in the clear, if harsh, light of reality and make the hard decision now.

This leads me to another point. If you want to succeed in business (or life), do not be conventional; sometimes you have to go against the grain.

The best investors in the world, including Warren Buffet, have a philosophy that goes totally against conventional thinking. Mr. Buffet says to invest in the market when everyone is selling and sell when everyone is buying.

This advice is from a man considered to be the most successful investor of all time and is currently worth $1.3 billion. Be the Warren Buffet in your field. Go against the tide. As some say, "Go big or go home."

Buckle up and enjoy the ride for the next part; I have never been a conventional person. Think outside the box? I don't even have a box!

Here's what to do.

If You Want to Keep the Success Wheel Turning

Spend 80 percent of your time with your High-Performers, those who are instrumental in your organization's success. This may seem contradictory since I have been saying not to micro-manage and leave your High Achievers alone.

No, do *not* micro-manage, but *do* spend your time motivating, inspiring, and strategizing on a high level, partnering with them in their and the organization's success.

Some of you are now scratching your head at this statement because it defies conventional thinking. *I do not think like most people.*

I imagine some of you probably spend much of your time helping people who need help the most, right?

Do not do this! You are wasting your time. Low performers are a drag on you and will always be that way. There is a reason they are low performers; it's in their nature and you cannot change them.

Please do not misinterpret me. I am incredibly compassionate and wish the best for every single person. But in terms of organizational success, it will be best if you surrounded yourself with the A-Team that is both coded for what they do and best intersecting with their passion and aligned with financial rewards.

Stop Being Afraid to Face Problems on Your Team

Managers are often afraid to confront things head-on and instead tend to be like ostriches and put their head in the sand and pretend a problem does not exist. Meanwhile, the hard-working members of the group that are getting all the work done are exasperated that nothing is being done with the low performer, which brings morale down for the entire group.

You then risk disenfranchising the group as a whole. Have you ever noticed that when that *one person* leaves the organization, you can hear a sigh of relief, and the energy in the room escalates?

You do not always need to outright fire the under-achiever. Have an honest and crucial conversation, including an exit strategy for that person or a plan to change positions. Sometimes a person is just is not a good fit for the job they're trying to do Give them an opportunity to excel in a different job or line of work within the company.

Many managers are too timid or not educated in the art of having crucial or difficult conversations and instead ignore them, hoping they will go away. My wife, who is an engineer, often says, "*Hope* cannot be your strategy."

I truly sympathize with those whose abilities are limited. I honestly do. But if you are a manager running a business or a unit within a company. In that case, you will need to make some difficult decisions and choices, but always in a fair, respectful, and compassionate manner.

I am reminded of the story of *The Frog and the Scorpion*, which goes like this:

One day, the frog was on his way home, and he happened upon a scorpion at the shore of a pond.

The scorpion said to the frog, "I'm fatigued today. Very tired. If it's not too much trouble, could you ferry me across the lake?"

The frog looked at him and said, "Mr. Scorpion, I would love to help you out, but you are a scorpion and I'm a frog, and surely, by the time I get to the middle of the pond, you will sting me, and I will die."

The scorpion said, "No! Mr. Frog, why would I do that? If I were to sting you in the middle of the pond, we would both surely drown! I cannot swim, and you are my only boat. So why would I do that?"

The frog thought about it and was a bit nervous, but being a good frog he decided to help the scorpion.

So, he scooted along the shore, the scorpion crawled on his back, and the frog started swimming, and when they got to the middle of the pond, the frog thought, "I guess the scorpion isn't going to sting me. What he said makes perfect sense."

Suddenly—*wham!*—he felt a sharp pain in his back. The scorpion had stung him.

Now the frog was struggling, his limbs and legs getting heavy, and he started to go under. "Why, Mr. Scorpion, why did you sting me? Now we will both surely drown."

The scorpion replied, "I don't know. I couldn't help myself. I'm just a scorpion and that's what we do."

This little tale offers a few morals and takeaways.

First, always trust your instincts. If it sounds like a bad idea, then it probably is.

Second, be aware that promises have consequences and carry the potential that the other person may backstab you.

If you have a weak, underperforming employee (or manager), find an exit strategy for them. Give them a time deadline to find the new job.

Those on the Margins

Look at it this way: Your marginal employees who need their hands held, make mistakes, and are not self-motivated. They were very likely unmotivated or under-achievers in school and throughout their entire life, and it's very unlikely you will get them to become motivated.

Please do not consider me a heartless person given what I'm saying about not helping low-performing or under-performing employees. On the contrary, I am highly compassionate and have the utmost sympathy. However, this book is about keeping your best to make yourself or your organization the best. You must help people, but eventually, charity work must stop to stay in business, or you will be out of business and not serving any good.

I always root for the underdogs; they are usually the most complicated working bunch. Low performers can be of a few different types and backgrounds. They either do not have the proper education, have some rough patches along the road, or want to succeed but have not been given the opportunity.

Or—yes, I'll say it—perhaps they are simply lazy with no motivation other than getting their next paycheck and going home and watching television or playing a sport or whatever it is that does not promote their potential excellence. These are the type of people that will not help your organization excel. Weed them out. If they are performing their delegated tasks as to their job description, then, by all means, you should keep them but do not promote them beyond their abilities.

Remember: *By spending time with low performers, you are putting your energy in the wrong place.*

Go with Your Highly-Motivated People

Being highly motivated, or an A-type personality, is built into someone, you, a part of their being, an innate characteristic. You either have it, or you do not. It is not something that can be learned.

Focus your attention on the best within your organization. It's a long-term strategy that will pay great dividends.

Spend most of your time and effort into training, coaching, and mentoring your highest achievers to make them even better. YES, it will provide incredible dividends overall.

That said, if the high-performers do not like to be micromanaged and do not necessarily need coaching, how will you spend your time with them?

Much of your work, time commitment, and strategy have to do with setting up training and development programs to make them even better. It would be best to show that you are engaged with them and want them to succeed. As the US Army's slogan proclaims, "Be all that you can be."

A-Types and high-achievers crave training and development. Develop training programs to provide the tools to excel even further. This accomplishes several things.

First, it illustrates that you genuinely care and strive for shared success.

Second, high-achievers will strive for even higher goals. All-Stars love to work hard and will bring you handsome rewards in new sales or clients.

Your top performers will understand that you are investing time and money into their professional development and demonstrating a vested interest in them. This, in turn, causes them to believe they can have confidence in you as a manager while also providing a reassuring sense of job security. "Why would they be investing all this effort into me if they don't want me around?"

Your high performers love to be involved in long-term planning and corporate initiatives. It would be best if you got them interested and engaged. A sense of purpose and a feeling of accomplishment resonates. Remember, these people are often driven by pure emotion. Always present the high-achiever with new challenges.

There were a few times when I was challenged with different initiatives that were not necessarily in our core line of business. People like me love challenges. Test us, challenge us, and your expectations will be wild-fully fulfilled. *We love a challenge!*

There were a few new business units that I was challenged to explore and, in the end, made significant inroads. This resulted in new projects, clients, and varying business ventures for the company. I loved it.

If you tell me or someone like me that we can't do it, well, by gosh, we will do it. I was a "B" student in school but, for the most part, worked harder than the "A" students, because people like me feel that we need to prove something. I craved experiencing a sense of self-worth and others' appreciation for a job well done.

As I said, I was a "B" student in high school, but when it came to my plumbing and HVAC apprentice-ships in the union, I won the award for being the top student all four years. I loved what I was doing. And I scored the highest score ever recorded on the Master Plumber exam, because I really loved what I was doing and was passionate about it.

Be Steady in Your Leadership

Because your top achievers *love* new challenges and initiatives—*but* it is essential to remember not to be willy-nilly in terms of changing directions.

Sure, it's possible in this rapidly changing business climate that you may have to make a strategic pivot. That's not what I mean here.

I have had managers and company leaders throughout the years who constantly changed their mission and initiatives. We would start a new project and gain momentum only to have the rug pulled out from under the project at the whim of the boss.

It was very demoralizing.

My peers and I would joke about it and call each new project or directive the "flavor of the month." It was like trying to hit a constantly moving target. We would say with a smirk, "Geez, what consultant did the president talk to this month?"

Constantly changing your brand or messaging or mission sends the wrong signal. It is recommended to evaluate your long-term strategy and goals yearly but be consistent in your messaging. Your people will get sick and tired of a constant state of rebranding or changes in the company culture.

If you want to avoid frustrating your best people, implement long-term thinking and strategy. Do not change your path too often, or people will get discouraged.

TAKEAWAY ... with a bit more insight

It does not take long to identify your highest achievers. Use the "Peter Principle" to continually challenge them with greater responsibilities to maximize their potential and see how high they can rise within your organization.

There will come a time when you observe when they have reached their potential. Be cautious not to promote them beyond that or they may fail.

Get to know their personality traits.

I, for example, have ADHD. My wife says that is what makes me so creative. It has both negative and positive impacts on me.

I have written, and am in the process of writing, several other books in various genres, including children's books, public speaking, and the story of miracles in my life. My mind does not work like most people's and I need to be constantly doing something different in order to feel engaged.

The three core symptoms of ADHD are inattention, impulsivity, and hyperactivity. My former boss could have used these traits to his advantage, but instead, he did not know how and could not handle me.

Some of these traits can definitely be used as an advantage. For example, I get work done very quickly and efficiently because I want to finish a particular task so I can move on to the next one.

I get bored very easily and constantly need new challenges. I could never do the same monotonous task day in and day out. People like me need to be constantly challenged with new tasks or opportunities.

Identify these types of people and constantly challenge them and you will have some of your best employees. Do not pigeonhole them. We love to tinker. I have a few inventions and helped my brother with an invention that he recently patented.

For example, one of the tasks I was challenged with at my old company was to set up a new division within the company. People like me thrive on this, and I successfully achieved this goal and brought in millions of dollars of revenue.

Lastly, being a great manager is like being a great sports coach. You cannot change people; don't waste your time. Instead, identify their strengths and weaknesses and manage them according to their traits and skillsets.

LESSON 7

Discipline

The so-called "unmanageable" are an interesting lot. I know this because I am their poster child. Our very nature seems to be freelance, but I have observed that when you craft concrete goals, we buy into them because we yearn to reach the "Promised Land" of the organization's best plan and highest goals.

Yes, a certain class of "unmanageables" can and will help you succeed.

Even so, you may sometimes cringe at their tactics, including coloring outside the lines. Keep your focus on results. Perhaps one of the best teachers of management is parenthood. Managing the unmanageable, at times, is like parenting children that are constantly testing their parents' boundaries. Remember that coloring outside the lines is how abstract art is formed and appreciated. The challenge is to give them enough room to excel without letting them go rogue on you.

Some Don'ts and Do's

Never chastise any employee in front of others. When you do, it's about your ego. You will crush them by humiliating them. Any manager worth their salt would never do this. At times, though, there must be discipline to keep order within the ranks. They sometimes flirt with the rules too much, testing the limits. This is not dissimilar to small children that test their parents to examine what their responses may be.

You cannot have anarchy, so don't allow it. You need systems—this is why management is an art. You need to know when it's time to stop painting.

When high achievers make new sales, gain new clients or projects, and consistently make money, you look good as their manager—but at times you may cringe at what they say or do. These "outside the lines" people can often have a potty mouth. This is unacceptable; don't allow it. If it happens, discipline them accordingly but fairly.

Here's what I advise: *Always praise in public and chastise in private.* This, I heartily believe, is a good rule for any manager and sound business (and parenting) practice.

With this in mind, know when to bite your tongue and when to deliver a well-deserved compliment. When an issue arises, have a serious conversation until the matter is resolved, even if it takes an hour or so to complete. Your "unmanageables" will behave better ... for a while.

The True "Unmanageables"

There is, of course, another type of "unmanageable"—the ones lacking motivation and who will not see that reaching goals is a great thing, personally and corporately.

The saying goes: "A tiger never loses its stripes," and the poor behavior of an "unmanageable" may continue. If it does, and becomes a pattern, you may need to go to the next step and deliver a documented, written warning. Usually, this is enough to make someone cool their jets and start behaving professionally.

If, however, the pattern continues and "the juice is no longer worth the squeeze," you will need to dismiss them regardless of how well they perform. I have suspended employees for a week or two without pay to give them time to ponder their actions. It usually works, at least for a while.

Most high achievers who are unmanageable take few vacations and bank the hours. Suggest they take time off. This will provide them with time to think about their behavior and possibly realize they really must change if they're going to thrive in their career. Consider it a cooling-off period for yourself, as well.

I have observed that this remedy will work in most cases if consistently poor behavior has escalated to this point.

Above all, watch for these misbehaviors.

Inappropriate Language and Actions

Any discrimination or sexual advances should have an absolute zero-percent tolerance level in your organization. Some, though, cannot or will not change. If such is the case, you cannot afford to have them in your organization.

Inappropriate behavior is a disease. Other things such as the constant use of foul language and telling crude jokes that may offend some people are less severe but still cannot be tolerated in the workplace. The offender must be disciplined appropriately. There needs to be a zero-tolerance policy for this type of behavior. This is not "Madmen" and it's not the 1950s.

In most situations, after a serious and stern conversation, they will get the point, understand the consequences, and be on the way to better behavior. If not, and they persist, they need to be let go.

TAKEAWAY

There is absolutely no room or tolerance for harassment or bigotry. Each and every person has the right to be treated with dignity and respect.

Your people will know if you truly value them for what they are, and not just checking a box for some corporate policy.

I have witnessed some horrific examples of sexual, ethnic, and religious bigotry and it makes me sick to my stomach. I imagine it was bad parenting. My parents taught us to treat the janitor the same as the Pope, and that you are neither above nor below any other person.

Set the bar high, and your employees will respect you for your integrity. Talk the talk and walk the walk.

LESSON 8

Learned in Egypt

I had been at a new and important job only about a month when my boss, the Senior Project Manager, dropped dead at his desk. There was a lot of concern and uneasiness about what would happen now. Would whoever replaced him be as good a manager?

Let me tell you, though that man was a good boss, what I learned by working for the man who replaced him has stayed with me the rest of my life.

Allow me to tell you about it.

What I Learned There

My wife and I spent several years in Egypt on engineering and construction projects. We had just gotten married two weeks before we left the U.S., and our assignments were in different cities. Did I mention this was our honeymoon?

We rarely saw each other because we were working in different cities on different projects. It was a day's journey from my project in Port Said to hers in Alexandria. Of course, it was challenging to be apart, but we each had our missions, all the while knowing we loved each other with all our hearts. Even so, we learned the truth of the saying, "Absence makes the heart grow fonder."

My wife is a successful and acclaimed environmental engineer, specializing in wastewater treatment, and she was assigned to a project in Alexandria. I was assigned as Mechanical Project Manager in a Port Saidat the beginning or end of the Suez Canal (depending on whether you are going north or south). I am deeply and madly in love with her since we met at a wastewater treatment plant and fell in love near a secondary clarifier, which separates biological floc from the treated liquid waste stream. How romantic is that?

I also had a project for a new wastewater treatment plant in Ismailia, which is in the middle of the Suez Canal, and a small village named Qantara, fifty kilometers south of Port Said. Qantara (pronounced *Antara*) is a small village where we constructed a water pumping station along with 50 kilometers of 60-inch pipe to send untreated raw canal water to the town of Port Said Water Treatment Plant.

The flat I had in Ismailia still had pock marks from .50- caliber machine gun bullet holes from the 1967 Israel-Egypt war. Unfortunately, there is still much hostility left over. (I wish everyone could love each other.)

Living in Egypt was, itself, a life-changing event for me. They have the best mangos I have ever had, and they taste like honey. I learned a lot about large construction projects and other cultures and perspectives. I had 120 Egyptian workers under me and soon discovered that they are among the kindest people in the world. They would give you anything they possess—a very hospitable people. I made a lot of good friends during my time there. Egyptians are kind to a fault. I tell you, the things I learned from that culture are second only to what I learned from what happened next.

A Whole Lot of Learning

As I mentioned at the start of this chapter, I had been in Port Said only about a month when my boss dropped dead at his desk.

Of course it was a sorrowful time with a lot of uncertainty After a few weeks, we were informed there would be a new Project Manager. Everyone was worried.

His name was Mr. Al, and he had a reputation as a rigorous person who managed a tight ship. It was reported that he fired *twenty-three* project engineers, superintendents, and project managers in just nine months on his last project.

Mr. Al summoned me from Port Said to the Cairo office shortly after his arrival. He was an older gentleman with a full head of silver hair and mesmerizing blue eyes, thin and of more than average height.

This would be his last project before retirement, he informed me, after working around the world constructing dams and pipelines for over 40 years. He had a long career with this multinational company and was greatly respected.

Mr. Al wanted people to perform at their very best. He told me he had what he called "The two-week rule." He would size you up in two weeks and terminate you if he did not think you were a high-performer and did not cut the mustard. He was not going to waste his time with underachievers. Under-performers were terrified of this man. I loved him.

Eventually, we became very good friends. Mr. Al told me he thought I was one of the hardest working people he had ever worked with, and was glad I was there to help him on this project that had gone sideways. I had his back and he knew it.

This project was a massive leap in my career, and [gosh darn it], I was not going to let Mr. Al down. This man was way out of my league, and I wanted to excel at my new venture. He managed billion-dollar construction projects.

When I arrived at the job, the mechanical portion of this $250-million wastewater plant was a year behind schedule. My predecessor was too busy playing softball and riding horses in the desert by the Giza pyramids, apparently unconcerned that the job was in absolute chaos and was delaying the entire project. I thought, *How can I ever fix this? I'm in way over my head.*

After just a few months, Mr. Al fired my co-worker Mechanical Engineer and sent him packing back to the States. I had to finish the other project he was commissioning and now had twice the workload. I saw that as another challenge.

It took me only a few days on the Port Said project site to realize that, though I was in a quagmire of dramatic proportions, I was determined to turn the ship around. Working seven days a week, things gradually did turn around, and within a year, we were ahead of schedule.

I thought, Gee, this is like working on the farm when I was a kid and I was trained to have a great work ethic. I had never overseen anything this significant before, and it was intimidating, but I was determined to please Mr. Al.

What I Had Learned as a Plumber Helped Me in Egypt

Like repairing a heat pump or figuring out how to solve a complex plumbing or boiler issue, the key is to break any problem down into small manageable pieces.

I've learned to pretty much fix any HVAC or plumbing problem, how to approach even the most complicate repair, and I applied the same techniques to get this project out of the black hole.

Here it is: Break it down. Solve one problem at a time. Tackle the most challenging issues first.

In my work as a plumber, I always had sticky notes (remember those days?), and I would put the day's most significant challenges on sticky notes, starting with the toughest ones first. I used different colors to provide me with a sense of urgency. Essential things were red, next was orange, then yellow. Less important problems or tasks were put onto the softer colors like greens and blues. This worked well for me. My mind works in technicolor. If I got through the yellow notes at the bottom of my priority list, I had a great day.

Prioritizing the tasks on this huge $250-million project helped me to start turning around what had been a production nightmare.

There was another key to turning it around, and that was how I treated the people working with and for me.

The People Factor

I owe a debt of gratitude to my Egyptian engineers who worked for me. All my engineers in the Cairo office were women, a group of amazing, smart, and talented people. I had the privilege of going to their houses for dinner and meeting their family, which meant the world to me. I was treated like royalty, as it was a big honor for them to have an American be their friend and a guest in their home—a very different cultural attitude than what I was used to, since, in America, "having people over" is not a big deal.

I would do small things for my engineers in the Cairo office, like buying them chocolate or taking them out to lunch on my bi-weekly visits there. This meant a lot to them, and I enjoyed being as generous to them as they were to me. In turn, they worked hard, and if there was a deadline for submittals or a proposal, they did not mind at all working overtime. I also got them raises to help their families live better.

The thing is, I had always taken care of my people. In Egypt, most of my field workers either did not have shoes or wore "shib-shibs," which are similar to flip-flops and are usually made of used tires.

My motto on the construction site has always been "Safety first." And since shib-shibs are not safe foot-wear for work, I ordered 120 pairs of work boots for my entire crew. The laborers and pipefitters were ecstatic, as they had never had a pair of boots before.

After about a week, I noticed that very few of my guys were still wearing their work boots and had returned to shib-shibs or were barefoot again.

I asked my chief Egyptian engineer what was going on. "Oh, Mr. Mike, that was a very kind gesture," he said, "but they do not make much money, and they sold the boots in the market for the money to feed their families."

Determined to make my crew safe, I came up with a plan. With the help of my chief engineer, who interpreted for me (my Arabic is sketchy, but I can get around), I gathered the crew and gave them the following plan.

For anyone who sold their boots, I would replace them, no questions asked. I would give those who did not, $35.00 US dollars. But this came with a stipulation. For those who kept their boots, I would bump their pay up 50 percent. If I ever saw anyone not wearing their boots, they would be immediately fired.

No one ever violated this rule during the rest of my time there.

As a side note: I also made them wear safety glasses and soon learned there was also a black market for that, but that's another story.

Another catch was that I needed them to work harder and more productive so we could obtain higher productivity rates. The plan worked with the blessing of Mr. Al, though he agreed to it with this stipulation:

After observing two months of labor productivity rates and statistics, he had better see a good increase.

My workers bought into the plan—but would they come through for me?

At the time, the minimum wage for an Egyptian worker was thirty-five Egyptian pounds per day, or about ten US dollars a day for public sector employees. For private employers, it was closer to twenty-five pounds a day. Then, one US dollar equaled 3.14 Egyptian pounds, which meant our average worker was making about $8 per day.

I bumped everyone's salary by 50 percent, up to thirty-eight Egyptian pounds per day from the standard twenty-five pounds. With 120 workers, this was an increase of about $890 US dollars per day in wage rates. The mechanical portion of the project I oversaw was approximately $80 million; in the grand scheme of things that amounted to diddly squat. My primary goal was to get back on schedule.

Our productivity increased by 50 percent, and we were back on schedule within a few months. Everyone from the civil and other crews wanted to work for Mr. Mike, the kind American. Word spreads. It did not cost us a penny more and gave my dear workers a better life. The pay increase was appreciated. It showed them I cared.

My guys were very loyal to me and treated me like a king. I would often jump down a ditch and show them how to cut pipe and put fittings together, perform startup on a piece of mechanical equipment, or drive a backhoe or loader—things I had always done in construction or on the farm. For them, seeing management or engineers doing any actual manual labor was something they had never witnessed before. It's not how their society works.

Earning Respect

The Egyptian workers were in awe when I would get in a ditch and get my hands dirty. (I had my safety boots on.) They could not believe it.

The point of telling this is that I earned their respect. And because of that, we finished the project with an outstanding safety record, on budget, and on time.

Always remember: No matter the culture or subculture, people need to be treated well and provided with a dignified life, a purpose, and a cause worth working hard for. They need respect. It grieves me when I hear managers and business leaders denigrate and disrespect employees because of their racial, ethnic, or economic background.

If you are loyal to your employees (your customers too), and treat them like you would your family, they will be faithful to you.

This is not rocket science.

Lessons from a Laundry Service

While in Egypt, you were expected to have a maid to clean your flat. In Port Said, I had two maids who were sisters and who came with the flat. Their full-time job was to clean my place. They did not get paid much; it was only a few dollars a day. I cannot imagine they worked very hard since it was only me living there, and I didn't make much of a mess nor do much cooking.

I ate out every night at the only restaurant in town with a menu in English. Oddly enough, it was called Hotel Cecil. There I made good friends with a group of Brits who were constructing tunnels under the Suez Canal to bring canal water to the Sinai Peninsula for irrigation. They were a great bunch, and I even became Godfather to the first child of my friend Alistair.

Booze was hard to come by, so my friend, whom I call Uncle John, taught me how to make beer. Uncle John was quite rotund and one of the happiest I have ever met. I loved that man. "Life is life" was his mantra that he would always say. He was casual and easygoing. I can't ever envision him getting mad or angry.

When Uncle John taught me how to make beer, he said, "The more sugar, the more the alcohol." So naturally, I doubled the amount of sugar in my first batch and waited for it to ferment.

About a week later, I came home from work and when I opened the door saw a lot of liquid on the floor coming from the pantry, where I had bottled all the beer. I opened the pantry door and was astounded at the amount of glass on the floor. The majority of the bottles had exploded. It was a disaster, and took hours to clean up.

I told John about this, and he asked what kind of bottles I used. I told him I just used whatever I could find. Well, come to find out, cheap old whiskey and soda bottles made of thin glass are not meant to hold the pressure. My first lesson in the homebrew world.

There was a note taped to the pantry door written in Arabic. I brought it to work the next day so my chief engineer could translate it. He started to laugh. The note said the maids would not come back until I got rid of the ghosts in the pantry that were breaking bottles.

Well, we got through that.

The maids would come during the day when I was at the project site. I rarely saw them. Neither spoke a word of English, and when they needed supplies, they would leave me a note in Arabic, I would have my Chief Engineer translate it for me, and he would have one of his guys pick up the requested supplies at the market for me.

Every week there was a need for a large box of laundry detergent. Due to the 100 percent customs tax on imported items, detergent was costly compared to what we paid in the States.

I thought it odd that they were using so much detergent and just figured that my crappy washing machine was inefficient and did not work well. I certainly did not go through many clothes. Heck, I can go a whole week with one pair of jeans.

One day, I got my first case of dysentery (I would get it two more times), and came home from work early. Imagine my surprise when I saw that the entire apartment was filled with hanging laundry. It looked like a forest of clothes.

I was too ill to even think about it and went straight to bed. Dysentery is awful. I feel so sad for the people who are not privileged enough to have clean drinking water. Clean water is taken for granted in the United States, Europe, and other parts of the world. Trust me; clean drinking water is a huge worldwide problem. It should be a fundamental human right.

The sisters were embarrassed, and they were running a laundry business to bring in extra income. After a few days of lying in bed, I returned to work and had my chief engineer write a note in Arabic to the maids.

I asked him to write, "Ladies, I know you think you are in trouble, but you are not. You are more than welcome to continue to do laundry for other people here. It will be our little secret."

My chief engineer said that they would have been fired or, worse, beaten if anyone else had caught them. My belief, however, is that we are meant to share the wealth we have with those less fortunate. Be kind and generous.

TAKEAWAY
- Treat employees—and for that matter, your waiter, or waitress, or plumber—as you would treat your friends and family. Don't be a jerk.
- Never ask anyone to do something you would not do. Be a servant leader and show by example. You will earn their trust and respect.
- Have compassion and empathy and show that you truly care for them not just as an employee, but as a person.

Why Some Managers and Employees Are Lousy and Why Some Are Great

Many managers are ill-prepared to manage in a genuine and effective manner. They may be the best engineer, banker, lawyer, or administrator, but most have had little proper and structured management training.

Most people specialize as a technician in their specialty field or trade but have little exposure to the art of management—and make no mistake, it is an art.

Primarily, people are often promoted to management positions because they have shown excellence in their profession. This is not a bad thing on the surface. Being an expert or highly proficient in your field, however, does not make you a competent boss, manager, or leader.

You may possess superior technical skills, but may lack the soft skills of management. There is a fear or no desire to manage well; they are forced to manage.

There are myriad unique personalities in the workplace, meaning that management needs to be prepared to deal with an entire spectrum of personalities and traits. There is no easy solution to this challenge, other than hard work and studying psychological behavior books to learn how the minds work and what motivates people.

An entire field is devoted to the study of workplace and employee psychology. It is not easy to be a stellar manager and leader. It necessitates studying and practice. Besides being highly proficient in your regular daily duties, if you intend to manage people effectively, you need to know:

- *What your company and customer needs are.*
- *How to ensure your subordinates have the skills to perform their tasks.*

- *How to provide employees a sense of status and recognition.*
- *How to develop an understanding of team cooperation within your group.*
- *How to conduct a frank and honest discussion on personal performance expectations.*
- *Straightforward ways of interacting with your team and providing a clear mission and goal.*
- *Experiencing and promoting a common bond with your team.*
- *Ensuring you give the team adequate resources to complete the tasks or mission.*
- *Mastering the ability to provide genuine praise when deserved and discipline when needed.*

And of utmost importance:

- *Know how to create a work culture where your employees cannot imagine working elsewhere.*

An excellent workplace environment tends to create an elevated level of retention and solid cohesion and collaboration within the team. This saves you an exorbitant amount of time, money, and resources by not constantly seeking out new talent.

I Have a Question

How many managers can you say you have worked for who had all or most of the skills outlined above in your career? Not many, I would venture to guess. They are a rare breed, and corporate America is full of mediocre managers promoted beyond their abilities.

It is important to praise all employees publicly. I am not suggesting that you should go around blowing a trumpet and making a big deal of it. The praise must be genuine and meaningful, mentioning specific achievements.

In the workplace, everyone talks, and in most organizations, there is a big rumor and gossip mill. The people participating in this behavior share many of the same traits as the lousy bosses and managers. I suggest self-examining and encouraging you to ask others if they think you have one or several bad characteristics or what area you could improve upon.

Many people tend to internalize things, and most do not have self-awareness. It is imperative to ask for honest feedback from your employees and peers.

Some Negative Traits of Lousy Managers

Lack of Clarity

A leader who lacks the ability to communicate clearly and who keeps changing their mind often is not healthy for companies.

I had one manager who regularly drove me insane. I would have a proposal nearly complete that I had been working on for months. At the eleventh hour, he twisted the whole thing around and changed the entire direction of the message and content I had developed based on my knowledge of the client or project we were pursuing.

This necessitated me spending all weekend rewriting and redoing many of the proposals. It was demoralizing. I knew it was a good proposal and a potential winner. However, it did not meet what *he* thought it should be. He would hint that he knew more than me, or so he thought. *Then why did you hire me?* I would think.

Feeling lost and useless was very discouraging. I would often say, "Why even try? He's just going to change the whole [dang] thing anyway?"

If you strive to be a great manager, please do not wait until the last minute to review something your subordinates have worked on for weeks or months and change everything at the last minute. It is very rude and inconsiderate behavior that provides for extremely low morale.

This is probably because the boss did not look at the project until the last minute, minimizing me and all my hard work. It was beyond frustrating, and all I wanted to do was quit and work for someone who did not procrastinate and wait until the last minute to do his job, who fulfilled his promises and didn't dump a bunch of crap on me—the one who completed his work on time.

Never Publicly Criticizing Employees

I mentioned this earlier, but it bears repeating, I believe, because I've seen it done too many times. Some managers have humongous egos and like to make themselves look good in front of their superiors while belittling others in public.

If you have to chastise an employee, do it gently and in private—remembering to praise loudly in public.

This practice builds a high level of morale within the team or group, earning you respect and loyalty.

Good managers realize they can approach you with an issue or a problem and will not be humiliated. It builds trust. Without trust, you have nothing but a house built on sand. It is only temporary and will crumble under waves of pressure.

The importance of trust cannot be stressed strongly enough. If your employees do not trust you, and if there is little mutual trust within your organization, you will not attain your potential level of greatness. *Creating trust* takes work and is earned. Be honest and be ethical in all your business practices.

Never Lie

As my mother used to say, "If you don't tell the first lie, you'll never need to tell the second." A trustworthy boss is the best boss ever. If you could trust that you can confide in your boss or manager your secrets, hopes, wishes, or dreams, would you not do anything in the world for that person? Of course, you would. *Be* that trusted manager.

Insecurity

I have had a few managers in my career who were highly insecure in their position, much to their detriment. I am a hard worker who strives for excellence, and I love to win.

Poor managers exclude certain team members from meetings that are important to that person's ability to do the job to the best of their ability. A lousy manager limits access to tools, information, and people and in so doing sabotages employees. Recognize a person's potential and empower them to succeed.

People do not leave companies; they leave their direct supervisors.

I have never left a company because I was not fond of the organization. The decision to depart was usually because my direct supervisor was a dud, jerk, or ass. Suppose there is just one thing to take away from this book: *Do not be the manager that drives people away.*

The unfortunate part about high achievers leaving is that often it leads to a domino effect. When a key player leaves, others wind up leaving, as well.

I fail to comprehend why, within the corporate world, constant employee turnover is not a huge red flag for managers. But often, upper/senior management tends to ignore it because Billy Bob or whoever it be, is consistently making money for the company. Senior leadership has blinders on in many cases, often foolishly ignoring the great cost of replacing employees.

Senior management usually does not wake up and come to their senses until they start losing profits, which is too late. Then comes damage control, consisting of a new company program, mission focus, and another coach or consultant to help put the pieces back together and stop the bleeding. And so the cycle starts all over again. I cannot fathom why these brilliant MBAs cannot grasp basic stuff.

I recently spoke with a great lady who held a high position at my former company. She was turning in her notice of resignation. I have also talked with a few other people within that firm, who are seriously considering leaving for the same reason. They all said, "If he fired you, a high performer, there's no reason he won't fire me."

Now, my former boss is doing damage control, putting out fires, and probably freaking out learning of imminent departures, which takes away from his productivity as a leader. Don't be that person.

Constant Micromanaging

When it comes to what *not* to do, micromanaging tops the list. High achievers do not need nor can they tolerate micromanagers. Period and exclamation point. They will leave. It is but a matter of time.

Instead, set annual goals and benchmarks for the year, which is managing macro- empirically. The goal may be in the number of sales, new clients, a dollar goal, or whatever metric is utilized. If a stellar employee meets or exceeds that goal, why would one microman-age them further? To squeeze out more profits? A need for control? I am not sure what drives this microman-agement. I am mystified.

Tangible goals are a must. If your employees do their job well if they meet or get close to the plan or purpose, you must let them conduct their part of the business the way they are doing it. High achievers are successful and strongly resent if a manager constantly looks over their shoulders and tells them how to get it done. But their behavior cannot weaken the foundation of the business platform.

Field-Tested

One good boss I had many decades ago put me in a position I'd never been in before. He was a very intim-idating person but had a good heart. He came across as very gruff, though I knew deep inside he had a heart of gold but did not like to show it. I imagine he thought it showed weakness in front of the rough-and-tumble construction crews.

My boss took me out of the field as a foreman and brought me into the construction trailer to do purchase orders, RFIs, equipment and material purchasing, and other similar tasks necessary to provide materials for the crews. I had never worked in an office before and was worried I would fail.

The tasks assigned to me were completely new and something I had never done before. My manager was a very busy person and did not have time to coach me, train me, or provide any form of mentoring. Whenever I had a question, his response would be, "Handle it. I trust your judgment." I did not ask many questions; I just figured things out on my own.

The new challenges made me want to strive to please him and do the best job I could with the new tasks. Those were the days before computers became popular, so I could not Google the subject or watch YouTube videos, which entailed going to the library to study up on the issues, and so I did.

I became so proficient at the new assignments that they transferred me to the main office to be a draftsman. I had never done drafting before and just had to figure it out. It was hand drafting. I got books from the library and studied up on how to be the best draftsman I could be.

Computer-aided drafting (CAD) was just getting started at that time. I felt proud of my accomplishments, and it gave me a desire to learn more. This was the launching pad of my career and enabled me to move up the ladder. I was an office jockey now. This was something I never really aspired to; I just kind of fell into it.

Trust Good Employees to Do Their Job

I worked for large corporations that charted revenues in the hundreds of millions and with some firms that did billions of dollars in revenue every year.

My sales goal for several years was $100 million/year in project wins. Some years it was $60 million, and in others $250 million, but I averaged over time meeting my goals. Can you imagine firing someone who brought in that type of revenue? I may have colored outside the lines, but I never blurred the line of expected professional conduct.

If I was bringing in new projects, I was autonomous, called my shots, and was incredibly happy. The company was making money from my effort. It was a win-win scenario. I never reported to an office but instead traveled extensively throughout the country. I had the freedom to call my shots and make my schedule. This was the perfect work environment for people like me to thrive and for me.

A later firm I worked for made the unfortunate mistake of micromanaging me and could accept my autonomous ways. This has cost them many tens of millions of dollars in revenue. They have already lost two projects that wanted me.

The owners of projects I was pursuing that my old company has since lost wanted *me*, not necessarily the company I was working for. What this reminds us is, any business is a people business. It is about the people. You have your favorite barber, hair stylist, plumber, auto mechanic, dentist, accountant, doctor, lawyer, insurance agent, and the like. When your trusted provider leaves a company, it is the norm that you will most likely follow them to their new place of business.

The Rewards of a $25 Cake

Until my insurance agent retired last year, he was my agent for nearly forty years. I often received letters and offers from other insurance companies, which could have saved me several hundred dollars a year. I was not interested. His name is Tim, and I knew I could always count on him.

Every Christmas, he would send me a delicious cake from Little Italy in Baltimore. It probably cost him $25. But do you have any idea how much that cake meant to me? Well, it was the world (and delicious). He remembered me and cared for me. And for that, he earned my loyalty. Whenever I had an issue or question, he took my call and gave me incredible personal service. And he was a nice guy, always accommodating and responsive.

Tim earned all my business, from car insurance, boat, homeowners, umbrella policy, business insurance, farm insurance. I would venture to guess that for over forty years, I have provided this insurance company with over $140,000 in revenue. I suppose the yearly $25 cake cost him about $1,000—pretty good ROI.

Why would I leave excellent personal service to save a few hundred bucks a year? That makes no sense.

The main reason you follow people and not companies is that you know them, trust them, and have built a relationship over the years that you want to continue. In most cases, it is not the company you care about but the person you interact with directly and trust their skills and their ability to solve your problems. You know the name of their kids, their significant other, and maybe even their birth date.

I deal with many engineering firms. I have witnessed some of their high performers leave the firm because they were dissatisfied, and their clients continued doing business with their trusted engineer and not the company they worked for before. The same holds for many businesses. It is about the people and the relationships they have built over the years.

Every company pays about the same price for a particular piece of equipment, technical services, or widget. Some buyers are driven strictly by price. If that is the case, there is no way you can persuade them to choose you over your competition unless you have the lowest price. Fire them as a client or customer. They are not worth your effort. Bring them value.

Many buyers value a trusted relationship with an outstanding employee or salesperson and are usually willing to follow them wherever they go. These are the clients you want and need. They are also the most profitable, and you will provide them with the best service possible.

When high-level achievers depart, the company loses much future revenue. Meanwhile, the competitor is thriving with all the new work Mr., Ms., or Mrs. All-star is bringing into their new firm through their relationships and contacts within the industry.

Put your pride aside and have the security of letting your top performers spread their wings and soar.

After all, that is the reason you hired them in the first place. They crave autonomy, so let them do their thing. Your best and most highly achieving employees have an innate ability and passion that you cannot control—Channel their knowledge and passion into positive results.

Delegate Tasks to the Right People and Find the Gems

How do you assign tasks to a person's skill set?

Identify the right person for a particular task or skill set needed. People do great in doing what they love to do, while they are not so proficient in performing tasks they disdain.

You may be surprised at the results of identifying the tasks in which employees will excel. In my career, I have encountered people whose undiscovered skills have surprised me tremendously once revealed.

I once hired a surveyor from West Virginia who had limited education and little experience in construction. His early career out of high school was blasting rock for coal companies at a strip mine. I was enamored with the stories of his blasting and how explosions tossed five-ton boulders in the air with dynamite charges.

He related one story in which he put too much gunpowder charge in the blast holes, sending a huge boulder flying for several hundred yards and landing on a car and crushing it. Fortunately, no one was injured, and he learned a powerful lesson that day.

I listened intently to his stories of working the coal mines and could see in his eyes that he had drive, vision, and a burning desire to exceed and be the best he could be. I observed that he had street smarts and a desire to excel. I was very fond of this kind and happy young man and respected his drive and perseverance. He was jovial and very forthcoming—the sort of person you want to be friends with.

My dad often said that success is 10 percent knowledge or ability and 90 percent perseverance and stick-to-itiveness. I firmly believe in that determining factor. That's why I do not dismiss anyone's resume based on just grades. I look for grit, determination, and drive to succeed. The "It Factor."

That said, look for those "B" students that worked hard to earn that B.

Look at their interests and activities.

Did they stick to playing an instrument?

Did they stick to sports or moto-cross or any activity that took determination and a fighting spirit?

You like to look for them as team players but also look for individual excellence, activities, and interests. You can hire those more than the over-achievers if that is what your organization needs.

"B" students tend to work harder. This is not a hard and fast rule, and you do not want your medical doctor, accountant, or attorney to have been a "B" Student. But in certain realms, like construction and service industries, I have found that hard work can overcome knowledge in many cases. People driven to succeed who have something to prove will find the answer.

The young man I refer to earlier kept wanting to receive new challenges. My colleagues and I went about piling on more different and challenging assignments for him. He studied hard and excelled at every unique opportunity. He is currently a top superintendent for one of the largest construction companies in the nation.

Do the greater, supportive work that keeps the company moving ahead.

I rarely even saw one of the best bosses I ever had; I will call him Mr. B. At a point in time, I was managing rather large construction projects all around the east coast, and I would see Mr. B only about twice a year. He would review the monthly financial reports and knew that my projects were profitable, with exceptional safety stats. In construction, safety statistics are a vital indicator of project success. If a project has workplace injuries, it is likely the project will not be profitable or organized. Never ever sacrifice worker safety over profits!

Mr. B just left me alone to do my thing. His visits were mainly just social. Mr. B would fly in on the company plane or jet, and we would have a nice meal. He and I would talk about everything. Religion, politics, family, golf, sports, and everyday stuff. I loved this man and still shed a tear thinking he is gone now. I was the guy he sent around the country to fix messed-up projects. The fixer and project-closer. Besides my family,

Mr. B was one of the most influential people in my life. I never wanted to disappoint him and make him proud of me.

Is that not the type of person you want to be? When you go to the next world, your employees will cry for you—the best treasure and reward. Mr. B knew my wife's and child's names and even their birthdays. Not many people were like that. He would send me a hand-written birthday or Christmas card. Be that person.

When Mr. B passed away several years ago, I flew to Atlanta to attend his funeral. I was no longer working for that company, but it did not matter. It was amazing how many of his former employees attended. This was such a testament to this fantastic and successful man.

Yes, of course profits and success are necessary in the business world, but in the end, it is only for a fleeting moment in time. Remember the big picture and realize what your legacy should be.

The Branson Touch

Another of the people I admire greatly is the founder of the Virgin Empire, Richard Branson. People love working for him. He is energetic and enthusiastic and treats his people well, letting them do their thing without micromanaging. This has made him remarkably successful.

Branson is known for his outstanding leadership abilities and the value he places on his employees. If every manager or business owner noted this, the world would be a better, more just, and peaceful place.

I love his statement: "You cannot be a great leader unless you generally care and like people. That is how you bring out the best in them."

TAKEAWAY

- Make goals achievable—ambitious but realistic. I recommend sitting down with your high achievers and together determine their yearly goals, whether it be in sales, professional development, number of new accounts, etc. Do not just randomly come up with yearly goals without their buy-in.

- Ensure that company policies and procedures are not too burdensome and do not interfere with productivity and serve a meaningful purpose.

- Provide support staff for the high achievers to assist with mundane tasks like expense reports and travel arrangements. This gives them more time to concentrate on what they excel in.

- Look for the diamonds in the rough—you may be surprised at their abilities. Challenge people with more and difficult assignments to determine if they are ready to rise to the next level.

- Provide an individualized touch by doing things like sending out birthday and holiday cards. It's a small gesture that costs little but demonstrates to employees that their manager cares about them as a person, not just as an employee. It takes one minute to send a card, and you have no idea how much this may mean to them.

If you are a high-level executive or an extremely busy manager, you may assign the task of handwritten notes or cards to a subordinate. The receiver generally will not know your handwriting. There are computer programs out there currently which can match your writing—a useful tool.

I encourage conducting social events outside of the workplace and inviting your employees' family members. It builds camaraderie and team cohesion. Events do not need to be fancy nor cost much money. Often, simple things and gatherings are the best and most memorable.

At times, poor managers engage in criticizing employees in public and displaying rude or insulting behavior. This translates into them not being able to motivate their team. Your business and productivity suffer as a direct result of this. The worst managers have low emotional intelligence and are out of touch with themselves and the real world. They typically cannot listen and control their emotions.

If you have this type of lousy manager or employee within your organization, rid yourself of them, because their behavior is toxic to the workplace culture. You will be happy that you did, and company morale will improve.

Know Your Audience

In the workplace, there are several generations of personnel, each with different skill sets, life experiences, cultural backgrounds, and needs. What drives the employees, and how do their minds work? What makes them tick and gives them satisfaction?

Let's examine the four generations in the workplace and describe their core characteristics. This is not a one-size-fits-all scenario but rather a consensus of certain traits. I fit into the first category, so my perspective may be skewed from yours. Like all of us, I am a product of my environment and upbringing.

Through conscious reasoning and talking to the other generations, I have made a point of seeing their perspectives in the workplace and life, which has made me a better, more compassionate, and understanding person.

Baby Boomers: Born 1946 through 1964

Boomers are retired or nearing retirement age. Their parents grew up during the Great Depression. They are generally careful with money and a bit cautious financially. They are achievement-oriented, competitive, and like to have status and titles. They tend to define themselves by their professional accomplishments.

Baby boomers are the most loyal group of all, and will provide stability to your organization. In general, they like to engage with people face-to-face or on the phone, so there is an interpersonal dynamic happening, and not through texting or email.

Many baby boomers are workaholics and resent Generation X and Generation Y people for what they assume is laziness and lack of work ethic. This group lived without cell phones, computers, or social media and are repelled by younger people who are glued to phones and computers.

Managing Baby Boomers

Baby boomers are big on goal setting and find self-worth in their achievements. Implement short and long-term goal setting to challenge them to be their best. Their desire to be the best frequently makes for incredible results for your company.

Help them with technology. Convince them that technology is their friend and will enhance productivity and make their job easier.

They did not grow up with modern technology. They are often reticent to ask for help and may need encouragement. Spend face time with them and interact in person. This facilitates conversation, creativity, and a high level of collaboration. Baby boomers tend to be religious. Bond over shared morals.

My parents grew up during the Great Depression. We were taught never to waste anything, to get as much education as possible, to work as hard as we can, and success will follow. Part of that is genuine.

The beliefs I learned from my parents still stick with me. Our mindset and life experiences mostly come from our upbringing.

Generation (Gen) X: Born 1965 through 1980

Gen X does not like to be micromanaged. They do not want or need approval with every project or task. They desire autonomy. Do not lean over their shoulders nor breathe down their neck. They will not last long in such an environment. They like to be engaged in finding solutions and want to be part of the process.

Gen X employees are motivated by things that offer them a good work/life balance, including family-based and lifestyle benefits. Unlike baby boomers, they generally do not believe in working overly long hours or dedicating their entire being to work.

Open communication is valued highly. Have an open-door policy for meaningful conversations. Being less averse to getting negative feedback, use that to your advantage to help them improve, and they will help a company be profitable.

They value being involved in projects they are passionate about. Generation X employees leave large corporations for small or startup companies where they think they will add more value and have independence and autonomy.

The primary drivers for them are passions for projects that interest them. They care about a company's culture and are interested in training and personal development. You need to know what motivates and retains them. They are soon to be the most significant portion of the current workforce. Doing so will have positive benefits to the company's bottom line.

I have a younger brother and sister that fit this category exactly, and I will say they are among the hardest workers I know. They are driven and passionate about their work and their causes. Both are innovative, creative, compassionate, and very successful. They were brought up on the tail end of the baby boomers but are, in reality, a different generation from myself and older siblings.

Millennials: Born 1981 through 1995

This group values loyalty, respect, and collaboration as top priorities. They, too, can be some of your best workers. Millennials want to learn and stay with an organization that allows them to utilize their skills and develop new ones so they are not bored or stagnant.

Many millennials are very good at completing projects expeditiously because they often develop creative solutions. They love to be in a collaborative environment, work with a team, and like input from multiple perspectives.

Once you gain the respect of a millennial, they tend to be very loyal to their supervisor and the company. If you support their needs, they will remain happy employees and stay for a long time. They like to be asked for their feedback and told of their value within the company. It gives them pride.

Putting them in a collaborative environment and being part of a cohesive team is crucial. This will make them thrive. Please provide them with feedback and ask for their opinions and suggestions on matters. You may be surprised at the great ideas they come up with.

This group likes to have autonomy and trust with a flexible work schedule. They want to work remotely part of the time but be in a team environment.

About 61 percent of millennials attended college *versus* 46 percent of baby boomers. They typically earn less than their parents, and the last recession struck them. They typically owe a lot of student debt. About fifteen percent still live at home. Only about 55 percent work in a field related to their college degree.

They are less likely to be homeowners than other generations. Sixty-three percent would have difficulty covering unexpected expenses of $500. This group is the least likely to become independent entrepreneurs. These are sad statistics.

My experience with millennials has been a bit rocky. Like the typical middle-aged guy, my opinion of these people has been slightly jaded.

I must admit that this generation has had it a bit rough compared to other cupcake generations. They currently number one-quarter of the population and are a strong force in the current workplace.

Generation Z: Born 1996 through 2015

The mindset of Gen Z can often cause conflict within the older generations. They grew up with computers, social media, cell phones, etc. Unlike old geezers like me, they know no other way, whose first computer was controlled by MS DOS commands using keyboard strokes. A mouse? That was some critter.

A little side story. My first computer was a 1985 Intel with 4megs of RAM. I wanted to run a CAD (computer-aided design) program for making construction drawings, and the memory was not sufficient to run the program.

Being ambitious, I purchased an additional eight megs of RAM for—now, get this—$1,200. Can you imagine spending that amount of money for 8 MB of memory? I wonder how many megs of RAM I could buy now for that amount of money. It is insane to think about now. 8 megs would probably cost a dollar now.

It makes me crazy that you can now buy a computer with 64 *Gigs* of RAM for less money than I paid for 8 Megs.

Back to Gen Z—they are addicted to technology. They are much more racially and ethnically diverse than previous generations and are typically children of millennial or Gen X parents and currently make up about 25 percent of the workforce.

Gen Z people are very open-minded and like to work in a diverse environment. They prefer texting over phones rather than having an in-person conversation. They are perfectly comfortable with Zoom or Teams and virtual meetings.

Gen Z wants to be with companies with a positive culture. They need to feel respected and valued. Your organization must have the latest technology and devices to retain these employees.

They tend to get stressed quickly with job security, work, and money issues. Probably nothing new you have not heard before, but they demand a job with a healthy work-life balance. This kills us as baby boomers.

Gen Z-ers prefer to work remotely and not occasionally report to a brick-and-mortar office. As a manager of Gen Z employees, one needs to create opportunities for growth and learning. Doing so gains your trust and makes them more loyal.

Instead of being mentored or experiencing in-person training, they prefer online training platforms like Udemy and Coursera for acquiring new skills. They are motivated by being able to voice their opinion and learning what type of training they need to progress in their careers. They like stability, which is good for long-term thinking and business longevity.

Gen Z workers demand career advancement opportunities, and you will lose them if your company does not have a program for internal promotions.

They prefer companies that promote from within and not outside hire. They bring value and offer a lot for companies in technology advancements. They are proficient at making tasks more straightforward and efficient using the latest technologies.

Why spend so much time focused on Gen Z?

Soon they will dominate the workplace, so one should do all they can as a manager to understand them and make them happy and satisfied with their career.

Bottom Line

Know your employee audience and their perspective on life and the working world. There is no cookie-cutter solution. It is no easy task managing different generations that hold varying goals, backgrounds, and religious and moral standards that can be on a very broad spectrum.

My advice is to get to know them personally and see how they function individually and as a team. Perhaps the younger generation would like to be mentored by an older generation. There can be great value in that, but you need to know your employees to determine if that will be helpful or detrimental.

I have mentored many young people in my career, and I get great satisfaction from doing so. But mentoring must be done gently, with compassion, and with a genuine concern for their career advancement and that of other human beings here sharing the same journey on planet Earth.

It cannot be just about you if you want to be truly successful. Show genuine concern and compassion.

Mentoring one or several younger folks will enable you to get to know them better and see things from their perspective. Without this interaction, it isn't easy to understand what drives them and what they want to achieve in the workplace.

Personal conversations and mentoring provide opportunities to realize their strengths and weakness and enable you to focus your efforts on areas that need the most improvement. Gen Z is our future, and their abilities and potential for achievement should not be underestimated.

Another side story: Several months ago, I spoke with a friendly young project engineer who was doing an estimating takeoff for a construction project. I asked him jokingly, "How many widgets did you count on that drawing?"

He looked at me with glazed eyes, revealing he had no idea what I was referring to. The only people who know the term widgets nowadays are the crowd over forty.

We were taught the term "widgets" in our Economics courses. I explained what widgets were, and we had a bit of a laugh. I did not realize I was so out of touch with some younger generations.

Now, widgets have gone the way of hoola-hoops, Evel Knievel stunt cars, Etch A Sketch, Hot Wheels cars, and phones with cords.

I have the utmost faith in the younger generations, and we must understand their perspective on life and society. Working with so many intelligent and capable young people has inspired me that the future does indeed look bright. They love to solve problems and make the world a better place.

Personally, I have had remarkable success with the young engineers. I cannot believe how bright and driven this group is, and we have had great fun in outside work events. They tend to crave knowledge and desire to learn and grow. There is hope for the world!

Workplace Bonding

I have been on many company retreats throughout my career. The most memorable was a cooking class for the group I was working with. At first, I thought it was stupid and silly. However, I did my duty and made the flight up to headquarters to attend the event.

This team-building event was held at a friendly resort in a peaceful setting at the edge of the mountains in New England. Our mission that day was to make linguine pasta, a sauce, and a dessert from scratch. None in the group were talented cooks, and we were all hesitant at first to make pasta, fearful we could not do so.

As it turned out, it was a blast! We succeeded in our goal of making pasta noodles from scratch, using just flour, oil, and water. Surprisingly it is a relatively simple task, and it sure beats the heck out of store-bought pasta. (The trick is to have a decent noodle-making machine.)

The team worked splendidly together, and by the end of the day, we were all laughing and having a great time. Everyone got a lot out of it, and we became closer as a group, bonding over food and cooking.

I worked remotely from headquarters and did not spend much time at HQ, so it was an excellent experience to get to know the team I worked with on a more personal level outside of the office.

For a small group or division within your company, I strongly recommend team-building experiences like this or something similar.

Another group-bonding experience was a fly-fishing trip on a scenic river with a beautiful mountain vista. None in the group had ever gone fly fishing before, and we had a fabulous time. The company hired a guide who taught us all we needed to know in a short crash course. I was fascinated by the whole experience and long to do it again.

Some of us even caught a few trout, which we pan-fried over a campfire and enjoyed immensely. Mmm, there are not too many better things in life than fresh trout cooked on a cast iron skillet over a fire!

TAKEAWAY

I strongly recommend team-building exercises at least yearly, especially if your group is working remotely as many are post-Covid. It builds camaraderie and trust. And trust is the bedrock and foundation of any successful organization. But one should be creative when planning these events. I strongly discourage the generic types that many firms utilize. Be different and unique and try things such as fly fishing, camping, cooking classes, a bake-off, beach volleyball, teams creating funny short animation films, etc. A great manager needs to know their audience and identify their personality traits and what gives them satisfaction within the workplace. Is it a title? Bonuses and perks? Simple respect

and working for someone who is honest and trustworthy?

Know what works to motivate and engender loyalty.

IN CLOSING

M anaging is hard. Managing is gratifying. You have to be a mother or father, psychologist, therapist, and referee to succeed. That is all on top of being technically competent in your field.

In closing, I would like to revisit some of the pointers and themes developed throughout this book; the ones you need most will leap out at you.

Manage the individual.

What makes them tick? Your management style should be tailored to provide the best, most productive working environment for a particular individual or group. There is no standard operating procedure nor play manual, but sound principles exist.

Have frank, sincere, earnest conversations with your group.

Ask them what they like, do not like, where they want to go, what drives them and how you as a manager or employee can help them to succeed. This is actual management, not just bossing people around and barking orders.

There is no one-size-fits-all approach to managing.

There is no "Easy" button. It is a rewarding experience to mentor and watch them grow, thrive, and move up the ranks.

Find the gems.

My dad used to say, "Never kick the water boy, for he could be your coach one day." I have found this to be perfectly accurate.

I often think about that great, young guy who was blasting for coal mines in West-by-Gawd, Virginia, and is now a very successful construction superintendent. Great managers look for diamonds in the rough and encourage them to advance and achieve their maximum potential.

I tried to hire him away, but he would not leave his company because they treated him well and leave him to do his job without breathing down his neck. I am glad he stayed.

The dividends of finding these diamonds are fantastic. They will help your company be profitable and a wonderful place to work. It is always a small world in any industry, and people talk. Whether at conferences, online or on social media, your company's reputation will be known as being positive or toxic. There is no avoiding this.

Become a company or manager everyone wants to work for, and no one wants to leave.

I am a great believer in *servant leadership.*

Never ask your employees to do anything that you would not do.

Your business is most likely different than mine, but many companies have certain similarities and things in common. None of us are too good not to pick up a piece of trash in a parking lot. A servant manager will always pick up the garbage. No one is beneath you, and no one is above you, as my mother would often say.

Being in construction and working my way up from a laborer to an executive position, later in my career, I would often visit job sites and, at times, would go down into a ditch to help a laborer with some shoveling or installing a piece of pipe. The laborers and craftworkers were shocked that I got my hands dirty but more in awe that I knew what I was doing. They had no idea of my background or training, just that I was some guy from the main office. Just some management guy.

The workers were surprised and amazed at this action, and I can confidently say that I gained their utmost respect and earned their loyalty. In their eyes, I was not just some figurehead in the office, and I showed that I genuinely cared about them and knew their daily struggles. Construction is hard work, as is farming.

Being a servant leader is a critical aspect of being a great manager. Show everyone that you care and always be respectful and kind. We should all treat the janitor just the same as one would the CEO, President, or Pope. It costs nothing to be the best boss or manager ever!

Treat people with dignity and respect, listen to them, get to know them, and care about them.

If you do these things, they will be loyal to you, and in turn, you will spend less time putting out fires and scrambling for new workers.

I have read countless management and employee motivation books throughout my career, and most did not inspire or leave me with any great takeaways. Some people tend to over-complicate matters. I like the KISS formula. Keep it Simple, Stupid.

Obtaining and keeping your A-players is a straightforward formula ...

... and most management books I have read woefully complicate the matter. Here is my simple recipe for work and life:

- Never lie—always be honest.
- Do not micromanage.
- Be trustworthy—trust in yourself and your employees.

- Never ask anyone to do anything you would not do yourself. (Be a servant leader.)
- Be humble.
- Be genuine—don't fake it.
- Show compassion and caring.
- Be generous.
- Remember the little things like cards, a personal note, a simple smile, and a hello.
- Treat your employees exactly as you would your family.

Lastly, remember that we are on this earth for only a short period. Make the most of it, and don't be mean or an ass. Your legacy will live on, so treat everyone with the kindness, respect, and dignity they deserve as fellow human beings.

Business success is not the be-all and end-all. While money and possessions are necessary, we are here but for a fleeting moment in time. What matters is how we treat everyone that we encounter.

Be a loving person, and people will love you in return and be loyal to you, helping you out in your time of need.

Live a life of contagious happiness and be the type of person that everyone wants to be around. Imagine yourself at your funeral. How many people from your place of work showed up? Did they have great things to say about you? Think about it.

Thank you for reading this book, and may peace and happiness surround you all of your days. By being kind, compassionate, and gentle with others, and your legacy will endure.

MOTTOS TO LIVE BY

On the other side of fear are magic and hope.
If you want to lift yourself up, lift up someone else.
—Ralph Waldo Emerson

If you come in second place, you are the first loser; silver medals only count in the Olympics.
Breathe in your courage, breathe out your fear.
Your rewards in life will be in direct proportion to the value of your service to others.
—Brian Tracy

Strive for progress, not perfection.
Act or accept.
Serving others prepares you to lead others.
—Jim George

Keep it simple; do not overcomplicate things.
Do unto others as you would have them do unto you.
It's not about trying to find something to help you be a
more effective leader. It's about trying to be a better person.

—James A. Autry

Any pain received today will be your strength tomorrow.
What we do for ourselves dies with us. What we do for
others and the world is, and remains, immortal.

—Albert Pine

Go to bed with dreams of success and wake up with a
purpose.
Attitudes are contagious; have a great one.
The best way to find yourself is to lose yourself in the service
of others.

—Mahatma Gandhi

Greatness is measured by courage and heart and love.
Do all the good you can do every day.
Opportunities don't just happen. You must create them.
We must be silent before we can listen. We must listen
before we can learn. We must learn before we can prepare.
We must prepare before we can serve. We must serve before
we can lead.

—William Arthur Ward

I have the power within myself to make me happy or unhappy today.

Have courage and be kind—always.

The greatness of a person is not in how much wealth he acquires but, in his integrity, and in his ability to affect those around him positively.

—Bob Marley

Carpe Diem. (Seize the day.)

Do no harm.

The true heroes of the new millennium will be servant leaders, quietly working out of the spotlight to transform our world.

—Anne McGee Cooper

To change the world, we must change ourselves.

It is better to light a candle than to curse the darkness.

Life is either a daring adventure or nothing at all.

Life's most persistent and urgent question is, 'What are you doing for others?'

—Martin Luther King Jr.

Vision without action is just a daydream.

Be more concerned with your character than your reputation because your character is what you really are, while your reputation is merely what others think you are.

—John Wooden

Live life on your own terms.
The meaning of my life is what I make of it.
Celebrate little victories. Every win matters.
Mistakes are simply learning opportunities.
Choose your battles wisely.

—John Thomas Cecil

Turn obstacles into opportunities.

—Anne T. Cecil

Find ways to step out of your comfort zone. Focus on success and love rather than fear.
I have never lost. I have either won or learned something.
Don't look to others for approval, find it within yourself.
You have what it takes to succeed.

—John T. Cecil

Learn what you can from others.
Never kick the water boy; he may be your coach one day.

—John Thomas Cecil

Gotta hay when the sun is shining.

—Grandma Rosie Cecil

Show yourself the same compassion you show others.

—Anne T. Cecil

You may not be able to save everyone, but you can love them.
—Anne T. Cecil

Be generous and live today as if there were no tomorrow.
Behind anyone's irritating behavior is a person. Always
be kind.
—Grandma Rosie Cecil

Living in harmony with others involves compromise.
Surround yourself with people who see the best in you.
A life spent helping others is a life with purpose.
—Mother Teresa

I am a work in progress; be patient.
—Mike Cecil

Be the kind of listener you wish everyone was.
Disappointment is an opportunity to practice patience,
gratitude, and flexibility.
Compassion is never wasted.
—Mother Teresa

We are more than our mistakes.
Never go to bed angry, always forgive anyone who has
wronged you.
—Anne T. Cecil

Right is right, wrong is wrong.

—Anne T. Cecil

Observe what is right; do what is just.

—John T. Cecil

ABOUT THE AUTHOR

Mike Cecil is the sixth of eight children and resides on a farm in Southern Maryland. He spent much of his youth on his Grandparent's farm in Saint Mary's County, where they grew tobacco and raised cows, sheep, and hogs. As a young lad, he sometimes worked in their country store. His Grandmother Rosie was the butcher and postmaster of Great Mills, Maryland.

After graduating from Mount Saint Joseph High School in Baltimore, he went to college, but he discovered it was not for him, so he entered the trades and became a Master Plumber, Master HVAC, Master Gasfitter, and Class B Master Electrician. He has worked in the construction field for the past forty-two years. The most memorable project was spending nearly three years on a large project in Egypt, constructing wastewater treatment plants and a water pumping station. He eventually went back to college night school and earned an associate degree in construction management.

His professional background includes spending nearly thirty years working as a plumber and HVAC mechanic, then as a construction superintendent and project manager, and finally as Director of Business Development for large construction contractors. He has given numerous presentations nationwide at conferences centered around the water and wastewater treatment industry. His flair for writing greatly helped him with the many technical proposals he has been involved with.

Throughout his life, Mike has spent much time volunteering for various charities and associations, including the Knights of Columbus, the Design-Build Institute of America, the Chesapeake Water Environment Association, and others.

He has always had a passion for writing but did not seriously think about putting pen to paper until he found himself without a job last year (the motivation for this book), and finally had some time to write several books. Other works in the process of editing and publishing include *Miracles in My Life, Grandma Rosie's School of Management,* and a four-part series about Nibbles the Cat, which is a children's book.

Mike considers his most memorable events occurring when he and his wife took a four-month backpacking trip around the world, visiting fourteen countries.

Some of the highlights of that trip included visiting Machu Picchu, taking a boat ninety miles up the Amazon from Iquitos, Peru, and hiking in the Scottish Highlands and the Himalayas in Nepal.

His hobbies include gardening, driving his John Deere tractor around the farm, and constantly working on home and barn improvement projects.

A free ebook edition is available with the purchase of this book.

To claim your free ebook edition:

1. Visit MorganJamesBOGO.com
2. Sign your name CLEARLY in the space
3. Complete the form and submit a photo of the entire copyright page
4. You or your friend can download the ebook to your preferred device

Print & Digital Together Forever.

Snap a photo   Free ebook   Read anywhere

Printed in the USA
CPSIA information can be obtained
at www.ICGtesting.com
JSHW022134080424
60804JS00002B/16

9 781636 982786